THE DARKLING PLAIN

THE
DARKLING PLAIN

A STUDY OF THE LATER FORTUNES
OF ROMANTICISM IN ENGLISH POETRY
FROM GEORGE DARLEY TO W. B. YEATS

BY

JOHN HEATH-STUBBS

EYRE & SPOTTISWOODE
LONDON

This book, first published in 1950, is printed in Great
Britain for Eyre & Spottiswoode (Publishers), Ltd.,
15 Bedford Street, Strand, London, W.C. 2, by
Jarrold & Sons, Ltd., The Empire Press, Norwich.

ACKNOWLEDGMENTS

Certain parts of this book have appeared in the form of articles in the following publications: The Penguin *New Writing, The Windmill,* and *Time and Tide.*

My thanks are also due to the following for permission to quote copyright material: Messrs. Heinemann, Ltd. for quotations from Swinburne's *Collected Poems*; The Oxford University Press and the poet's family, for quotations from Gerard Manley Hopkins; The Oxford University Press for quotations from *Selected Poems of Richard Watson Dixon*; Messrs. Methuen and Co., Ltd., for a quotation from *The Vicar of Morwenstow* by S. Baring-Gould; Messrs. Macmillan and Co., Ltd., for quotations from Wilfrid Scawen Blunt, and Hardy's *The Dynasts*; Mrs. Martha Clare Stallibrass, for poems by John Clare; Mr. Edmund Blunden; The Society of Authors, as the Literary representatives of the Trustees of the Estate of the late A. E. Housman, and Messrs. Jonathan Cape, publishers of his *Collected Poems*; Messrs. Gerald Duckworth and Co., Ltd., for quotations from C. M. Doughty's *The Dawn in Britain*; Messrs. A. P. Watt and Son, Mrs. W. B. Yeats, and Messrs. Macmillan and Co., Ltd., for some lines from *Dialogue of Self and Soul,* quoted from the *Collected Poems of W. B. Yeats.*

I have also to thank many friends who have helped me by their criticisms and suggestions, particularly Mr. David Wright for assistance in collecting biographical material.

J. H-S.

CONTENTS

INTRODUCTION

THE purpose of this book is not so much a historical survey, as an attempt towards a revaluation of the poetry of the later nineteenth century, or rather, of certain lines of development to be found there. I am concerned with the later fortunes of what, for the sake of convenience, I will call the Romantic tradition in English poetry. "Romantic" as a term in literary criticism may be applied, first of all, as opposed to "Classical", to certain elements of style and subject-matter, which may be discerned in the work of many different writers at very different periods. The term is a relative one, and, of course, there is no such thing as a purely "Classical" or "Romantic" writer. Thus we speak of Greek tragedy as being essentially a "Classical" art form, in contrast with the "Romantic" drama of Shakespeare and his contemporaries; yet Euripides may be legitimately spoken of as a Romantic when compared with Aeschylus and Sophocles. One poet may be Classical in the restraint and regularity of his style, and belong to a Classical tradition and culture, yet have a strong undercurrent of Romantic feeling as, for example, with Virgil. Another may be Romantic as regards his subject-matter and his treatment of it, yet a criticism that looks below the surface may discern in him an essential Classicism, both of style and outlook—Ariosto is a case in point. For a Frenchman, Corneille is more Romantic than Racine, yet an English reader would probably find his plays far more austere than those of Dryden, who is the great initiator of the Classical period in our poetry. Similarly, Goethe is called a Classicist by German critics and historians of literature, though by English standards he is probably as much a Romantic as Wordsworth or Coleridge.

Nevertheless, I believe these terms, Classical and Romantic, to be not merely convenient labels, but to have a real critical significance. Within the historical context of the development of European literature (which from Homer to our own day is a self-conscious unity that has never really been broken) they correspond to two different modes of expression of an imaginative response to the universe. The Classical vision is the most complete, rounded, and perfected of which the limited human mind is capable; it is life, as Matthew Arnold said of Sophocles (who is perhaps the nearest to being a purely Classical poet that we know), seen steadily, and seen whole. In a sense, we must all ultimately attempt to be Classicists, but we have to be Romantics first of all, before we can achieve this; and few of us, in this life, can hope to pass that stage. For Romanticism is dynamic, the movement towards the clear integrated whole; it belongs to the world of Becoming, rather than of Being. Historically, it is a symptom both of growth and of disintegration. There is one sort of Romanticism which belongs to the beginning of a culture, before it has attained to its classical maturity; another sort which manifests itself as a reaction against a Classicism which has become a mere system of dead conventions, artificially superimposed upon the imagination. It is this dynamic nature of Romanticism which makes its characteristics so difficult to define. Nostalgia for the past and repudiation of the past, extreme idealism and crude realism, a preference for subjects taken from familiar and humble life and a preoccupation with the exceptional and the fantastic, Christian mysticism and atheistic humanism, belief in democracy and exaltation of the aristocratic idea, faith in human perfectability, and the profoundest pessimism—all these, however contradictory, were equally characteristic of the Romantic movement of the late eighteenth and nineteenth centuries. It is during this historical period that the Romantic response to the universe most clearly and completely dominated European art and letters, and we are therefore justified in applying the term "Romantic" in a secondary, historical

sense, and in a general way, to a certain style or way of
writing, which was dominant at this time. It is the successor
to the other post-Mediæval styles which we can identify in
the historical development of European literature, and, by
analogy, in painting, architecture, and music as well. These
we may conveniently term the Renaissance style (represented
in England by the Elizabethan), the Baroque (which dominated the first half of the seventeenth century), and the
Augustan or Classical, characteristic of the late seventeenth
and of most of the eighteenth century. In our own century
the Romantic style has been superseded, largely, by a new
style, as distinct from it as it was from any of its predecessors;
this, for the present, we must be content simply to term the
Modern style.

But in the history of English poetry the term Romantic
is, strictly speaking, only applicable to the poets who
flourished during the last decade of the eighteenth century,
and the first three of the nineteenth. These are great names
—Wordsworth, Coleridge, Byron, Shelley, and Keats, with
Blake, though in some respects anomalous, as in many ways
their forerunner. This was a turbulent and revolutionary
generation; the poets were largely made vocal, indeed, by the
idealism and the hopes which the French Revolution of 1789,
and the revolutionary wars which followed, called forth,
though Wordsworth and Coleridge were later to wean themselves from the aspirations of their youth. Even Keats, who
of all of them seems to be most preoccupied with purely
aesthetic experience, was politically a Radical, and in
Hyperion he treated, under the guise of the myth of the conflict between the Titans and the Olympians, of the super-
session of an outworn world order by a new and higher one.
But in the world of poetry alone, these men succeeded in
sweeping away the canons of taste that had dominated the
eighteenth century, and creating a "shift of sensibility"
which, within their own lifetimes, gradually altered the re-
sponses of readers. This shift in sensibility prepared the way

for the Victorian poets, of whom, by general consent, Browning and Tennyson are the two most typical and significant figures. The style of Tennyson's early work, for instance, is essentially a continuation of the style of Keats, though, before the publication of his first volume of poems in 1830, he had passed through phases in which he had assimilated the work of Byron and Shelley as well.

Yet it is obvious that a gap, of feeling and stature, as well as of time, separates these Victorian poets from their Romantic predecessors. The temper of the Victorian Age was very different from that of the High Romantic period. Prosperous and peaceful, it was outwardly of less violent and revolutionary temper than had been the earlier decades. But the rise of science, and of a materialist philosophy which laid claims to a total explanation of the universe, produced profound internal conflicts, and a disintegration of long-accepted religious ideas. Much of the poetry of the Victorians, in contrast to that of the earlier Romantics, is a poetry of doubt and questioning. The writers feel themselves to be on the "darkling plain"—

Where ignorant armies clash by night

envisaged by Matthew Arnold in *Dover Beach*.

The prime motive force of the Romantic movement had been a revolt of the intuitive imagination against the rationalism and empiricism of the eighteenth century. This revolt led the poets to the rediscovery of Nature as a living power, standing in an organic relation to Man, and of the imagination itself as a shaping, creative force. Mythology, which had been reduced to a merely decorative function, or, more consistently, rejected altogether by the Augustan poets, was rehabilitated. The gods and dæmons of poetic fancy became, in Shelley and Keats especially, the living incarnations of the forces of the subconscious world, whose existence psychology was just beginning to divine. Fundamentally, this process was a rediscovery and a transvaluation of religious symbolism, though only in the work of Blake was this phenomenon explicit.

No such shift of sensibility separated the work of the Victorian poets from that of the earlier Romantics as it did that of the latter from the eighteenth century, or that of the Victorians from the poetry of our own day. But though style and subject-matter remained largely the same, there was a radical weakening of this imaginative, mythopœic quality. The idealism of the earlier period was replaced by a mechanistic and materialist view of the universe, which the most typical Victorian poets strove to counter by a search for an intellectual faith. This, in the case of Tennyson, took the form of an argued hope for the gradual progress of humanity, and for personal immortality. But this is continually contradicted, especially in his best verse, by an imagery expressive of melancholy regret for the past, guilt, and unsatisfied longing:

> . . . but most she loathed the hour
> When the thick-moted sunbeam lay
> Athwart the chambers, and the day
> Was sloping towards his western bower.
> Then, said she, "I am very dreary,
>   He will not come," she said;
> She wept, "I am aweary, aweary,
>   O God, that I were dead!"

The optimism of Browning is more emphatically than consistently or convincingly expressed. From an intellectual point of view, he has been criticized for ignoring the existence of evil. But an examination of the actual imagery and subject-matter of his verse reveals a mind continually drawn to a contemplation of the dark places of human experience. With no characters is he more commonly occupied than the moral or artistic failure and the hypocrite, and he has an almost pathological obsession with crimes of violence and cruelty. *The Ring and the Book* is a laborious and desperate attempt to find ultimate truth in the history of such a crime, and its final conclusion is little more than—

> This lesson, that our human speech is nought,
> Our human testimony false, our fame
> And human estimation words and wind.

This lack of integration, of harmony between the conscious and the unconscious aspects of the personality, is, I think, particularly characteristic of the Victorians, and, among the poets of the time, it is seen most fully in Tennyson and Browning. It is in this that they fail to continue the poetic tradition initiated by the earlier Romantics. For though their work is full of romantic elements, they fail, as a rule, to relate them organically to the central impulses of their poetry. This is most clearly seen in the *Idylls of the King*, where Tennyson utilizes the traditional cycle of English legend, whose possibilities for epic treatment had allured poets of the stature of Milton and Dryden before him. With a few exceptions—the descriptions of the last battle, and of Arthur's passing, in the *Morte D'Arthur* itself (which belongs to Tennyson's early period), are noteworthy—he failed signally to bring out the underlying, archetypal significance of the ancient mythological symbols he was employing. In Coleridge's *Ancient Mariner*, Shelley's *Alastor*, or Keats's *Endymion* and *Hyperion*, on the other hand, we are continually aware of the presence of such symbolic significance attaching to the pattern of the plot, and the mythological and quasi-mythological figures that move through it.

It is for this reason that, in considering the development of Romanticism in English poetry after the death of Byron in 1824, it has seemed to me better to forgo any attempt to estimate the work of Browning and Tennyson, except incidentally. I do not wish to detract from their merits—though, in the case of Browning, I have never been able wholly to convince myself that these are, in many cases, strictly *poetic* merits. But if we omit Browning and Tennyson from our picture of the later nineteenth century we are in a better position, I think, to see the tradition of Romanticism expressing itself along certain other lines of poetic development.

In general, it seems to me, intuitive Romanticism, finding itself confronted by the bleak materialism of the industrial age, and an atmosphere of increasing doubt and spiritual insecurity, maintained itself among certain poets who were, in one way or another, outcasts from their time, and untypical of the main tendencies of Victorian literature. It is with the work of these poets that we shall be mainly occupied in the following pages. Towards the end of the century, the Romantic impulse re-emerged in the poetry of the pre-Raphaelites and their successors, but it had now become bound up with a doctrine which limited the scope of poetry to the sphere of purely aesthetic experience, so that it abdicated its right to speak, as the earlier Romantic poets had spoken, with a universal relevance to contemporary human destiny. Nevertheless, this movement preserved, and to some extent enlarged the Romantics' intuitive consciousness of the nature of poetic symbolism, and of the inner life of the unconscious from which poetry has its being. Hence it was that out of this aesthetic poetry there emerged, at the end of the century, in the person of W. B. Yeats, a poet who was able to recapture for Romanticism that sense of the realities of the objective world which it had lost. His work forms the link between the poetry of the nineteenth century and that of our own day.

I have considered poetry as a species of mythology or significant dream. And for this reason I am more occupied with the implications of a poet's imagery, symbolically interpreted, than with his explicit "philosophy of life". But such an approach renders it necessary to consider his personality as a man, and the social and economic context in which he wrote. I have accordingly included, in the present work, a certain amount of biographical information, but only as much as seemed relevant for my purposes, and for the most part, only in relation to those poets whose life and works are not very well known.

I have confined myself to poetry, and to that poetry which seemed to me to have imaginative significance. The period covered by this book was prodigal of verse of second-rate or third-rate artistic merit. Much of this might well be used to illustrate the tendencies of the time, but at the deeper level at which I have attempted to work, a consideration of such verse did not seem to me to be necessary. Though the scope of this book roughly corresponds to the Victorian period, I am concerned with the Romantic tradition, rather than with what is specifically Victorian.

I have attempted some sort of a revaluation of several well-known names, and have sought to rescue, for serious criticism, others which have been generally neglected, or relegated to the status of "curiosities of literature". In general, I have tried to consider, in some detail, the work of all the poets who seemed to be germane to my subject, and to group them so as to show the various courses by which the Romantic tradition strove to perpetuate itself in the hostile atmosphere of the Darkling Plain. One or two poets, however, it seemed better to omit, as they could not well be fitted into such a treatment. Thus the work of Emily Brontë, both in verse and prose, might be taken as representing a peculiar development of the earlier "Gothic" and Byronic Romanticism, in the hands of a woman of genius, acting under a force of inspiration which might better be termed dæmonic possession. But her position is such an isolated one, and the consideration of her work raises such specialized psychological problems, especially in relation to its origin in the "Gondal" saga of her childhood, that it seemed more convenient to ignore her.

Another, and very different case is that of Edward Fitzgerald. His influence was important, for he provided the "decadent" poets of the end of the century with a philosophical poem, expressive of a sensual pessimism, which might be taken as complementary to the emotionally mystical hope voiced, for the preceding generation, by Tennyson in *In Memoriam*. Fitzgerald, moreover, imported into Victorian poetry what was sorely needed—something of the ease and grace of the eighteenth century. But his work presents complex and delicate problems for the critic. Fitzgerald's sensibility, like Beddoes and Housman, seems to have been largely homosexual. All three of them felt a psychological or social compulsion to wear a mask in their poetry. Beddoes donned the mask of an archaic form, Elizabethan tragedy, Housman that of a ballad simplicity which only served to conceal the complexities of the personality which lay behind his poetry. In Fitzgerald's case the mask was translation. Free as his version of Omar Khayyam is, it is impossible to say how much he sunk his own personality in the original. Moreover, the mediæval Persian poetry which was his source was itself a poetry full of evasion and ambiguities. It is the product, perhaps, of a secret tradition, developing in clandestine opposition to rigid Moslem orthodoxy. Wine, love, and flowers, in this poetry, are now images of sensual enjoyment, now symbols of mystical experience; but, as often as not, I suspect, both meanings cohere together in them, in a way not easy for our analytical intellects to grasp. Something of the same ambiguity seems to have entered into Fitzgerald's paraphrase, and makes an objective consideration of his work difficult.

THE DARKLING PLAIN

Chapter 1

THE DEFEAT OF ROMANTICISM

BEFORE 1825, Byron, Shelley and Keats were dead; Wordsworth and Coleridge had largely ceased to produce work of first-rate interest. A decade or so was to elapse before the reputations of Tennyson, and later, Browning began to be established. The first blaze of Romantic poetry in England seemed to have burnt itself out; an insipid prettiness, a shallow sentimentality, a lifeless classicism, or, above all, a heavy didacticism, marked the most popular poets of the interregnum—The two Montgomerys, L. E. L., "Barry Cornwall", Mrs. Hemans, Talfourd, Sir Henry Taylor, and the rest. Even the greatest of the Romantic poets had often written carelessly, tediously, or in rank bad taste; but with the 'thirties and 'forties a quality of fustiness fell upon English poetry which we can only characterize (perhaps we are prejudiced) as peculiarly Victorian. For it remained even when Tennyson and Browning had revived something of the old spirit. These last two poets undoubtedly possessed fine qualities of imagination, but there is a lack of harmony between their imaginative intuitions and their intellectual convictions, which gives to even their most exquisite work only a flawed and limited perfection. The narrow scientific materialism of the age and the short-sighted social ethic of utilitarianism stifled the finer Romantic protest, which had so courageously reacted against the empiricism of the eighteenth century. A poet could no longer allow his intellect and emotions to work together and remain acceptable to the great mass of readers.

Yet these opening decades of the Victorian era saw the mature development of three poets whose natural place was in the succession of the Romantics, rather than with their

Victorian contemporaries and successors. Darley's work received a little, though limited, recognition during his lifetime. Beddoes left for Germany; such a man as he, indeed, could hardly have found a place in the England of his time. His work is largely fragmentary; we can only conclude that an inner sense of isolation and futility forced him into a laboured remodelling and writing over of *Death's Jest Book* throughout the greater part of his life. Most of his poetry remained in manuscript, locked away—the fact is symbolic— in Browning's bureau, like a suppressed memory in the mind. Hood's works on the other hand were widely read throughout the century, though during his lifetime he had to struggle against miserable poverty. But it was the album-verses, sentimental and comic, he turned out to buy food for himself and his family, which were so popular; not the few splendid poems in which his genius preserves its integrity.

Each of these three men, it seems to me, had at least as much potential poetic power as Browning or Tennyson, yet they were unable to weather the troubled seas of the nineteenth century, while the younger men were to gain positions of general public esteem. The explanation, I believe, is this: Browning and Tennyson, like good Victorians, achieved a compromise—though at a great spiritual cost. By conniving at the divorce of intellect and emotion, they were able to dispose the images, often passionate and terrifying, which their Romantic imagination bodied forth, in such a manner as to disarm them of their significance—as mere embroidery to conventional and prosaic themes. These themes, in reality, held no inspiration for them however much they might deceive themselves. By such means they were to render poetry palatable—Browning to the earnest Puritan intellectuals of the day, Tennyson to the vast new middle-class reading public—as never before. Besides, there was another factor—that of economics. The "hungry 'forties" seem to have produced a slump in poetry, which affected several of the more promising writers of the time. Industrialism, also, was producing a new leisured class which was, perhaps, less discerning in matters of taste than its predecessor—though the exact part which this factor played in the decline in aesthetic standards which marked the Victorian Age is not, I think, so easy to estimate as one might think. The growing Puritan temper of the time, and the reaction which Byron's life and personality induced in the years following his death, also told in favour of conventionally didactic or pious verse, as against more imaginative writing. Now, though neither Browning nor Tennyson in their early years was in affluent circumstances, they were nevertheless in possession of sufficient private income to be able to devote themselves entirely to poetry, even though that poetry was neglected by the public. This was not the case with Hood and Darley, both of whom were forced to dissipate their energies in journalistic work. Darley was also diverted from literature to the more profitable study of mathematics, as was Beddoes to that of medicine.

The merits of Darley and Beddoes, and of Hood's serious poems, are now generally recognized; yet I do not think their work will ever be widely popular. Compared with that of their Romantic predecessors there is a morbidity, a love of the strange and grotesque, above all a harshness in their imagery and conceptions, which is repellent to normal minds. Keats, the last born of the great Romantics, is the poet to whom all three, in the richness of their imagery and the acuteness of their sensuous perceptions, are most akin. Yet there is a striking difference between the atmosphere which breathes from the work of the later poets and that of Keats. If we examine their imagery it is possible, to some extent, to analyse this atmosphere. The mighty deserts and heaths of Darley's *Nepenthe*, the fantastic mythological and animal figures of the same poem, the cold "syren" which appears so often in his minor lyrics, the images of physical decay which throng upon us in Hood's *Ode to Autumn, Haunted House, Last Man*, and other poems, above all, the ever-present skeleton and death-symbolism of Beddoes, are among the factors which give to their poetry an aura of harshness, strangeness, and sterility.

Contrast with this the impression left upon the mind by Keats's poetry. It is one of a sensuous richness, a rounded softness, yet at the same time of abundant vitality. His work is crowded with images of growing vegetable life, of rounded fruit and flower forms; in addition certain objects of human workmanship—cups and urns—make a frequent and significant appearance in his verse. Of the first type of image are "The wealth of globed peonies" of the *Ode on Melancholy*, the swelling gourd, ripened apples, plump-kernelled hazels of the *Ode to Autumn*; of the second, are "the beaker full of the warm south" of the *Ode to a Nightingale*, the Grecian Urn itself. These are random examples—a systematic examination of Keats's imagery would reveal many more. A psycho-analyst would class them as female symbols. Their preponderance in Keats's poetry is not, however, any mark of a strong feminine element in his psychological make-up; indeed the reverse. They are called forth rather by his strong and normal masculinity—by his frank surrender to the allurements of feminine roundness and softness, conceived objectively, and their emotional concomitants. It is a surrender which many sensitive natures, subjected to an atmosphere of constant mental stress and uncertainty, are not strong enough to make. This, I believe, explains the harshness in the imagery of Darley, Beddoes and Hood—Romantics born too late into an uncongenial world. In this connection the probable homosexuality of Beddoes, in some ways the most typical and perhaps the greatest potential artist of the three, is highly significant. I hope to show that an analysis of it will go far to explain much that is characteristic both of his life and of his work.

George Darley was an Irishman, born in Dublin in 1795, the eldest of four brothers and three sisters. His father, Arthur Darley, a rather feckless character, came of a family of architects and builders. He married his cousin, Mary

Darley, who was remarkable both for her beauty and her musical talent—which last most of her children inherited. George Darley, however, does not appear to have been particularly attached to his mother, whom he mentions, in one of his letters, as lacking in sympathy. It is worth mentioning that one of his sisters, Anne, became, after her marriage, the mother of the actor and playwright, Dion Boucicault.

From shortly after his birth until the age of ten, Darley was brought up by his grandfather, as his parents had gone to America. It was during his childhood, apparently as the result of an illness, that he acquired a stammer which was severely to affect the course of his future career, making him abnormally nervous, and something of a recluse.

In 1815 he entered Trinity College, Dublin, as a pensioner, and in 1820 took his degree, but failed to obtain a fellowship. His stammer was an obvious bar to his success in most of the professions, and he went to London, having determined to earn his living by his pen. He had brought with him enough money to publish a book of poems at his own expense, and made the acquaintance of such literary figures as Lamb, Miss Mitford, Barry Cornwall, and Monckton Milnes; and also met, among others, Beddoes and Clare. But in a letter written at this time he complains: "Want of funds, of introductions, of speech and address, of worldly knowledge and dexterity— of (last but not least) *brains*, has kept me and will keep me a *poor* author . . . I am not a *genius*." On another occasion he says: "I write for self-entertainment, and perhaps to afford the world, after I have left it, some notion of what strange beings may pass through it without its knowledge." All Darley's poetical ventures were printed at his own expense, and *Nepenthe* was merely circulated privately among his friends. His doubts of his own ability to succeed in literature led him to devote himself to the study of mathematics. He published several mathematical text-books, and one astronomical treatise. These were sufficiently remunerative to allow him, in 1830, to travel in Italy and France, where he attained sufficient knowledge of the arts to become, in his later years, a leading art critic. He died—apparently of consumption—in 1846.

Darley's principal poetic ambition appears to have been to succeed in the drama, and ِhe failure of his *Sylvia* to attract attention seems to have been a great blow to him. His ideals were similar to those of Beddoes, whose *Bride's Tragedy* he admired. He was, however, rather surprisingly, indifferent to the work of Keats and Shelley. Byron, especially the latter's dramas, aroused his detestation. He described him as: "A lady's poet—all romance, and heroism, and elopement, and love, and death, and sentiment, and all that." In an open letter addressed to Byron he called him: "The greatest enemy of poetry your country ever had. . . . To your genius I ascribe the manifest debasement which now pervades this department of our literature [the drama]. . . . You had skill sufficient to dilute our native poetry to a kind of melting influence." There is, I think, a great deal of justice in this criticism. Though the early Victorian age was to witness a reaction against Byron's individualism and dæmonic *persona*, a great deal of what was worst in the poetry of the period must be traced to the influence of his diffusely grandiloquent style. In Darley we seem to discern an independent mind, running in many things counter to the tendencies of his age, but without sufficient strength or confidence in himself to establish his position as a rebel.

One poem of Darley's is well known. *It is not Beauty I Demand* was mistaken by Palgrave for an anonymous seventeenth-century lyric, and included as such in the second book of the *Golden Treasury*; thus it still stands in some editions. In other anthologies it has been the most frequently reprinted of the author's poems:

> It is not beauty I demand,
>   A crystal brow, the moon's despair,
> Nor the snow's daughter, a white hand,
>   Nor mermaid's yellow pride of hair;

Tell me not of your starry eyes,
 Your lips that seem on roses fed,
Your breasts where Cupid trembling lies,
 Not sleeps for kissing of his bed:

A bloomy pair of vermeil cheeks,
 Like Hebe's in her ruddiest hours,
A breath that softer music speaks
 Than summer winds a wooing flowers,

These are but gauds; nay what are lips?
 Coral beneath the ocean stream,
Whose brink when your adventurer sips
 Full oft he perisheth on them.

And what are cheeks but ensigns oft
 That wave hot youth to fields of blood?
Did Helen's breast though ne'er so soft,
 Do Greece or Ilium any good?

Eyes can with baleful ardours burn,
 Poison can breathe that erst perfumed,
There is many a white hand holds an urn
 With lover's hearts to dust consumed.

For crystal brows—there's nought within,
 They are but empty cells for pride;
He who the Syren's hair would win
 Is mostly strangled with the tide.

Give me, instead of beauty's bust
 A tender heart, a loyal mind,
Which with temptation I could trust
 Yet never linked with error find,—

One in whose gentle bosom I
 Could pour my secret heart of woes,
Like the care burthened honey-fly
 That hides his murmurs in the rose,—

My earthly comforter! Whose love
So indefeasible might be,
That when my spirit won above
Hers could not stay for sympathy.

The melody of this, and the genuine wit of some of the lines, might well have been struck out by Carew or other of the Caroline lyrists. But there is an excess of contemplative sensuality in some of the images, and a touch of sentimentality in the closing stanzas, which betray the poet of a later school, intellectually more undisciplined. Nevertheless, it is a favourable specimen of Darley's work, which includes, besides miscellaneous lyrics, two pseudo-Elizabethan chronicle plays —*Ethelstan* and *Thomas à Becket*, the pastoral fairy-play *Sylvia*, and the *Dramaticules*—interesting dramatic *scenas*, likewise in the Elizabethan manner. The bulk of this is *pastiche*; but some modern critics have been too ready to use that word in a purely derogatory sense. At its best, *pastiche* may lead to the genuine recovery of a valuable mode of poetic feeling which has been lost.

But there is one poem of Darley's—the two cantos of the unfinished *Nepenthe*—in which he reveals himself as a highly original writer, and in the direct line of succession from Keats and Shelley—and also from Blake. There is no other poem of like length in the English language which possesses such a continuous intensity of lyrical music and vivid imagery. Written in the four-stress couplet of *L'Allegro*, varied by the introducing of more complicated stanza forms, the whole poem, though narrative in subject, is really one intense, breathless lyric, hurrying the reader on with a truly Dionysiac inspiration.

Nepenthe belongs to a class of poems very characteristic of the younger Romantics—the symbolic dream-poem; a *genre* which owes its popularity, probably, to the revival of interest in Chaucer, Petrarch, and Dante. Of this sort are *The Triumph of Life*, the prologue to *The Revolt of Islam*, and *The Fall of*

Hyperion. The subject and plan of *Nepenthe*, however, links it rather to another type of poem, employed by Shelley and Keats, of which *Alastor* and *Endymion* are examples. In these, as in *Nepenthe*, the hero, who is the poet's ideal self, passes through a diversified dream-landscape in the continual quest of some symbol of satisfaction and integration. In this case it is for that Nepenthe which is at once the symbol for poetic inspiration and the life-giving fluid which is sought in the wilderness of emotional and spiritual frustration. The knowledge of the symbolism employed by the subconscious mind which the writings of Freud and Jung have opened up to us, reveals a new interest and value in these dream-poems of the Romantics, where fields of thought and experience beyond the waking consciousness are explored through the medium of the poetic imagination.

Darley himself, in a letter to a friend, furnishes only the following hint as to the interpretation of *Nepenthe*: "The general object or mythos of the poem," he says, "is to show the folly of discontent with the natural tone of human life. Canto I attempts to paint the ill effects of over-joy; Canto II those of excessive melancholy. Part of the latter object remains to be worked out in Canto III, which would likewise show—if I could ever find confidence, and health and leisure to finish it—that contentment with the mingled cup of humanity is the true 'Nepenthe'." But we should beware of treating this somewhat commonplace scheme, suggested, it is probable, by *L'Allegro* and *Il Penseroso*, as furnishing more than a consciously deployed scaffolding for a poem so crowded with brilliant images and strange evocative symbols.

At the opening of the poem, the hero finds himself upon a sunlit heath:

> High on his unpavilioned throne
> The heavens' hot tyrant sat alone,
> And like the fabled king of old
> Was turning all he touched to gold.

The glittering fountains seemed to pour
Steep downward rills of molten ore,
Glassily tinkling smooth between
Broom-shaded banks of golden-green,
And o'er the yellow pasture straying
Dallying still yet undelaying,
In hasty trips from side to side
Footing adown their sleepy slide
Headlong, impetuously playing
With the flowery border pied,
That edged the rocky mountain stair,
They pattered down incessant there,
To lowlands sweet and calm and wide.
With golden lip and glistening bell
Burned every bee-cup on the fell,
Whate'er its native unsunned hue,
Snow-white or crimson or cold blue;
Even the black lustres of the sloe
Glanced as they sided to the glow;
And furze in tasset frock arrayed
With saffron knots, like shepherd maid,
Broadly tricked out her rough brocade.

This fiery, solar imagery pervades the Canto, as in the second part watery and lunar symbols predominate. The hero remains in contented enjoyment of the sunlight and flowers, and is lulled to rest by the song of a brook. Suddenly the Eagle, bird of Jove, swoops down upon the dreamer and carries him off, as it had once carried off Ganymede. This image is taken from Dante's *Purgatorio*, Canto IX (a reference later in *Nepenthe* to the region where "Eden high, With terraced stairs that climb the sky, Long lost to mortal ken doth lie", proves, I think, that Darley had been reading the *Purgatorio* when he wrote his poem). The same image, also elaborated from Dante, forms the central *motif* of Chaucer's serio-comic *House of Fame*. In that poem Chaucer, leaving the Temple of Venus (which suggests the subject-matter of his earlier Allegories) loses his way in a desert of sand. Thence he is carried by the Eagle to the Temple of Fame, which is crowded with people of various sorts and conditions. Here he is to hear "tydings of Loves folk". It hints, perhaps, at Chaucer's entry into the new and wider world of the *Canterbury Tales*. If we compare the three instances of the image in the different poets—Dante, Chaucer, Darley—we may conclude, I think, that in each case it represents a moment in the author's development as a poet. Hitherto he has been content in the enjoyment of the sensuous world about him, but suddenly he is conscious of his destiny as a poet as a force more than personal, carrying him onward and upward to the intenser exploration of fresh fields of experience. The Eagle is this force, seen as the messenger of God, Jove's thunder-bearer; and also, imperial bird of the Roman legions, as the embodiment of the historical tradition which stands behind the poet, linking him to his great predecessors.

The Eagle in *Nepenthe* carries the hero to Arabia, where he beholds the continual burning and rebirth of the Phœnix. The lyrics which describe this are amongst Darley's best known and some of his finest:

O blest unfabled Incense Tree
That burns in glorious Araby,
With red scent chalicing the air
Till earth-life grow Elysian there!

Half-buried to her flaming breast
In this bright tree, she makes her nest,
Hundred sunned Phœnix! when she must
Crumble at length to hoary dust!

Her gorgeous death-bed! her rich pyre
Burnt up with aromatic fire!
Her urn, sight-high from spoiler men!
Her birth-place when self-born again!

> The mountainous green wilds among
> Here ends she her unechoing song!
> With amber tears and odorous sighs
> Mourned by the desert where she dies!

This is the first of the two "symbols of proud solitude" which are of central significance in the poem—the second being the Unicorn, which is introduced at the end of the next Canto. The Phœnix, Darley tells us, signifies "melancholy gladness"; it is the self-consuming energy of the Pride of Life. Having tasted a drop of its blood, the hero is at first overwhelmed by intoxication. He sees approaching a band of Nymphs or Bacchantes, images of sensuous pleasure, and joins their frenzied revel. The passages of the poem which follow are full of a wild vitality such as are to be found nowhere else in English poetry. The "over-joy" whose ill-effects were to be shown in this Canto may be interpreted as an excess of masculine, outgoing energy, which first abandons itself to sensuous pleasure, and then rises into an overweening ambition. Ida, the abode of the Gods, towers up before the hero, and he hurries forward to scale it. But a warning voice is heard; it is a dirge for the drowned youth, "sky-rejected Icarus", punished for his soaring pride, whose body now floats down the Dardanelles:

> In the caves of the deep—lost Youth! lost Youth!—
> O'er and o'er, fleeting billows! fleeting billows!—
> Rung to his restless everlasting sleep
> By the heavy death-bells of the deep,
> Under the slimy drooping sea-green willows,
>   Poor Youth! Lost Youth!
> Laying his dolorous head, forsooth,
> On Carian reefs uncouth—
>   Poor Youth!
> On the wild sand's ever-shifting pillows!
>
> In the foam's cold shroud—lost Youth! lost Youth!—
> And the lithe water-weed swathing round him!—

Mocked by the surges roaring o'er him loud,
"Will the sun-seeker freeze in his shroud;
Aye, where the deep-wheeling eddy has wound him?"
    Lost Youth! Poor Youth!
Vail him his Dædalian wings in truth,
Stretched there without all ruth—
    Poor Youth!—
Weeping fresh torrents into those that drowned him!

The image of the drowned man is one of peculiar poignancy which haunts English poetry whenever the poet envis-
ages the possibilities of failure, through the overreaching of
his powers. While he remains master of his own creative
impulse, the poet may be said to ride that sea, which is at
once the welter of his subconscious emotions, and the surge
of impersonal hostile forces which surround him in the world.
Should his genius fail him, he may at any time be sucked
under, and become the sport and prey of unco-ordinated
passion within, and the world's cruelty without. The image
here particularly suggests Lycidas, under the whelming tide,
visiting the bottom of the monstrous world, beyond the
stormy Hebrides washed far away, whom Milton lamented in
such a personal sorrow, a symbol of the poet defrauded of
Fame's achievement by mischance. It is significant that from
T. S. Eliot's Phlebas the Phœnician onwards, the image is
repeatedly found in modern poetry. Now, as never before,
the task of preserving his integrity is rendered difficult for the
individual; and the temptation to give up the struggle, to
allow the waters to go over his head, is powerful. In this
connection, the actual manner of their deaths in the case of
Shelley, among the Romantics, and of Hart Crane, among
the poets of this century—in the former case possibly an unconscious, in the latter a deliberate suicide by drowning—
were perhaps more than mere chance.

But the hero of *Nepenthe* is deaf to the warning. He con-
tinues in his wild career, till the enjoyment of Elysium seems
to be within his grasp. Then reaction comes. The Nymphs

3

are changed into Erinyes—a somewhat obvious piece of allegory this: the torments of conscience and shame succeeds to sensual indulgence. They pursue him with wild cries.

> "Hollo after!—to living shreds tear him!—hollo after!
> To the ravenous wild wind share him!—hollo after!
>> Our rite he spurns,
>> From our love he turns,
> Hurl him the glassy crags down! hollo after!
>> With your torches blast him,
>> To the broken waves cast him,
>> Head and trunk far asunder!
>> With a bellow like thunder,
> Hollo after! hollo after! hollo after!

And the Canto closes with the following remarkable metrical effect, without parallel, I think, in the whole of poetry and akin to that produced by counterpoint in music. The dirge for Icarus and the Furies' chorus are blended in the ear of the drowning man:

> In the caves of the deep—Hollo! hollo!
> Lost Youth!—o'er and o'er fleeting billows!
> Hollo! hollo!—without ruth!
> In the foam's cold shroud!—Hollo! hollo!
> To his everlasting sleep!—Lost Youth!

The second Canto opens with a lengthy invocation to Antiquity. The poet is confronted by the vision of monuments of superhuman and primæval grandeur—pyramids, cyclopean ruins, colossal structures—of the ancient east and south, of the New World, of the Celtic and barbarous north. These are the "Asiatic vague immensities" of Yeats's line, and they usher in the exploration of "excessive melancholy"—the pride of solitary and indrawn self-contemplation. In this Canto the imagery is Apollonian, as that of the former had been Dionysiac, though it is not the Sun, but the female figures of the Moon and the Dawn Goddess, who are here the presiding influences. The plan is less definite, and the lyrical element less prominent, than in the earlier Canto. The dreamer awakes in the valley of the Nile:

> As from the moist and gelid sleep
> Of death we rise on shuddering bones
> The waste of that long night to weep,
> Which[1] pined us down to skeletons;
> So shuddering, weeping, weltering, worn,
> Gleaming with spectral eyes forlorn,
> Upon my bleak estate and bare
> Greyly I rose . . . .

> .   .   .

> Air
> Hangs like a hell-blue vapour there,
> Streaming from some thick ooze, that cold
> Over my foot like reptiles rolled
> Sluggish, with many a slimy fold.

In these lines and those which follow, Darley gives us a momentary glimpse of a Hell of sexual shame and impotence, not unlike the "slimy sea" of *The Ancient Mariner*. However, he is aroused by the sorrowful but loving song which arises from Memnon's statue, as the light of his mother, the Dawn Goddess, falls upon it. Follows the account of the hero's tracing the Nile to its source in the Mountains of the Moon —that is, perhaps, the poet's following of the stream of introspective, melancholy thought to its subconscious source in the mountains of lunar intellectual self-contemplation. Here he is able, by an act of charity, to free Memnon's spirit from its clay-bound state, though his own is still doomed to wander in the deserts of melancholy. It seems probable that Darley's allegory is here directly influenced by that of Keats's *Endymion*. This passage may be equated with Endymion's under-water wanderings. The figure of Memnon is similar

[1] *The Muses' Library* edition of Darley's poems reads: *We*, which does not appear to make sense.

to that of Keats's Glaucus, and the act whereby the hero of
Nepenthe frees the former, so that he is reunited to the Dawn
Goddess, corresponds to that by which Keats's hero brings
about the reunion of Glaucus and Scylla, and restores to life
the drowned lovers. In *Nepenthe* the hero proceeds on his
journey, to be finally confronted by the Unicorn, the image
of the Pride of "most majestic sadness":

> Lo! in the mute, mid wilderness,
> What wondrous Creature?—of no kind!—
> His burning lair doth largely press,—
> Gaze fixt, and feeding on the wind?
> His fell is of the desert dye,
> And tissue adust, dun-yellow and dry,
> Compact of living sands; his eye
> Black luminary, soft and mild
> With its dark lustre cools the wind;
> From his stately forehead springs,
> Piercing to heaven, a radiant horn,—
> Lo! the compeer of lion-kings!
> The steed self-armed, the Unicorn!
> Ever heard of, never seen,
> With a main of sands between
> Him and approach; his lonely pride
> To course his arid arena wide,
> Free as the hurricane, or lie here,
> Lord of his couch as his career!—
> Wherefore should this foot profane
> His sanctuary, still domain?
> Let me turn, ere eye so bland
> Perchance be fire-shot, like heaven's brand,
> To wither my boldness! Northward now
> Behind the white star on his brow
> Glittering straight against the sun,
> Far athwart his love I run.

The third Canto, which was to point the mean between
these two estates of pride, was never written. Indeed, I doubt

whether Darley, who seems to have been a lonely, nervous and disappointed man, could have achieved that synthesis which the completion of the poem demanded. Nevertheless, *Nepenthe* remains a highly original and valuable contribution to the imaginative survey the early nineteenth-century Romantics made of the world of interior experience. It is also a poem of considerable technical interest; the freedom of its metrical plan, its sharp transitions and its vivid use of dream imagery, anticipate much that is characteristic of the poetry of our time. This interest is sufficient, I hope, to justify the somewhat disproportionate length of the analysis I have given it.

In the work of Darley, we can see Romanticism pushed to the limits of normal experience. In that of Thomas Lovell Beddoes, his junior by eight years and the profounder poet, we pass beyond those limits, into a world of strangely fascinating, though often perverse beauty.

It is unfortunate that Beddoes is one of those writers to whom a label has become attached. He has been called "the Last Elizabethan". The phrase has stuck, and has influenced most modern criticism of this poet. The mistake could only be made by a reader who studied the later Elizabethan dramatists superficially, with an eye to their more sensational imagery, rather than to the view of life which lay behind it. There is little that is really Elizabethan in Beddoes, except the outward trappings of his dramas. It is true that he handles dramatic blank verse with a technical mastery, and possesses, perhaps, something of that "unified sensibility" which Mr. Eliot has detected in the Elizabethans, to a degree rarely found in poets who wrote since the seventeenth century. But his blank verse is written with a self-conscious artistry foreign to the early dramatists, and the quality of his poetic thought is entirely different from theirs. Both Beddoes and the later Elizabethan (or, more properly, Jacobean) dramatists are obsessed by the idea of Death; but it is precisely here that their attitude and his differ most fundamentally. The outlook of Webster, Tourneur and the rest[1] is inherited from the tradition of Mediæval Christianity, with its *Danse Macabre*. Death is the wages of Sin: Death the Leveller. However much physical dissolution is dwelt upon, it is feared and hated as a horror and indignity:

> Does euery proud and selfe-affecting Dame
> Camphire her face for this? and grieue her Maker
> In sinfull baths of milke, when many an infant starues
> For her superfluous out-side, all for this?
> Who now bids twenty pound a night? prepares
> Music, perfumes, and sweete-meates? All are Husht.
> Thou maist lie chast now! it were fine, me thinkes,
> To haue thee seene at Reuels, forgetfull feasts,
> And Uncleane Brothells! sure 'twould fright the sinner
> And make him a good coward, put a Reueller
> Out of his Antick amble,
> And cloye an Epicure with empty dishes.
> Here might a scornefull and ambitious woman
> Looke through and through her self—see Ladies, with false formes
> You deceiue men, but cannot deceiue wormes.[2]

In contrast to this, in Beddoes's treatment of Death, there is, blended with the feeling of repulsion and horror, a softer emotion of sensual, we might well say sexual, tenderness:

> Is it not sweet to die? for what is death,
> But sighing that we ne'er may sigh again,
> Getting at length beyond our tedious selves;
> But trampling the last tear from poisonous sorrow,
> Spilling our woes, crushing our frozen hopes,
> And passing like an incense out of man?
> Then, if the body felt, what were its sense,

---

[1] Ford is, perhaps, a partial exception. He comes closer to the later Romantics, and the resemblance which his verse and imagery bear to that of Shelley has often been noted. The lines from *The Witch of Edmonton:*

> All life is but a wandering to find home,
> And when we're gone, we're there

are typical of Ford's approach to the idea of death.

[2] Tourneur: *The Revenger's Tragedy.*

Turning to daisies gently in the grave,
If now the soul's most delicate delight
When it does filtrate, through the pores of thought,
In love and the enamelled flowers of spring?

Beddoes passes beyond the "easeful death", which could
be called "soft names in many a mused rhyme" of Keats—
that ceasing "upon the midnight with no pain", the Death
which is "life's high mead"—to a fuller realization of that
state of merging, in dissolution, with the beauty of the natural
universe which Shelley envisaged in *Adonais*. He enters a
region of thought and feeling not often explored in English
poetry; though it is one with which the German poets, from
Novalis to Rilke, have been familiar.

In one form or other, the death-wish pervades the poetry
of Beddoes; now a shadow, moving grotesquely, as a skeleton,
or in the misformed and dwarfish shapes of his clowns; now
striding forth in images of strange and terrible power. Sometimes Death is seen as a state of mystical and transcendental
union with the Universe; now it woos the poet's soul, gently,
like a lover:

> A ghost, that loved a lady fair,
> Ever in the starry air
>   Of midnight at her pillow stood;
> And, with a sweetness skies above
> The living words of human love,
>   Her soul the phantom wooed,
> Sweet and sweet is their poisoned note,
> The little snakes of silver throat,
>   In mossy skulls that nest and lie,
>   Ever singing, "die, oh! die".

> Young soul, put off your flesh, and come
> With me into the quiet tomb.
>   Our bed is lovely, dark and sweet;
> The earth will swing us, as she goes,
> Beneath our coverlid of snows,
>   And the warm leaden sheet.

Dear and dear is their poisoned note,
The little snakes of silver throat,
In mossy skulls that nest and lie,
Ever singing "die, oh! die".

A similar intense preoccupation with death is found in the work of Beddoes's contemporary, Poe. Here it is pretty clearly the expression of what the psychoanalysts would diagnose as an obsession with the womb, and a desire to return to the prenatal state. We have only to remember Poe's preoccupation with the theme of premature burial, and the highly personal use he makes of the conventional "Gothic" machinery of vaults, dungeons, etc. But with Beddoes, at least, this is not the whole story; his imagery is at once more intensely sensuous and more intellectual than Poe's. It arises from a far deeper conflict within the soul. He is the most Germanized of English poets, and voices that longing for extinction itself, at once passionate and abstract, which seems, in Germany, a country which has been first divided physically within itself, and then more tragically given over to the despotic leadership of men themselves neurotic, to have penetrated deeply into the communal consciousness.

During his lifetime Beddoes published only *The Improvisatore*, a miscellaneous collection of immature verse, and *The Bride's Tragedy*. During the rest of his career he prepared tentative collections of verse for the press, and continually revised *Death's Jest Book*. Besides this play and *The Bride's Tragedy*, four others remain in an incomplete condition—*Torrismond*, *The Second Brother*, *The Last Man*, and *Cupid's Arrow Poisoned*. The last two, though consisting only of disconnected fragments, nevertheless comprising some of his finest work. His range is, of course, narrow, and he has no contact with the emotions of common experience as they are normally understood. In his pursuit of grotesque and novel effects he is not secure from self-conscious sensationalism. But at his best, these faults are outweighed by the vividness and intellectual suggestiveness of his images—such images as this, from the fragments of *Death's Jest Book*—of a subterranean city:

> I followed once a fleet and mighty serpent
> Into a cavern in a mountain's side;
> And, wading many lakes, descending gulphs,
> At last I reached the ruins of a city,
> Built not like ours but of another world,
> As if the aged earth had loved in youth
> The mightiest city of a perished planet,
> And kept the image of it in her heart,
> So dream-like, shadowy and spectral was it.
> Nought seemed alive there, and the bony dead
> Were of another world the skeletons.
> The mammoth, ribbed like to an arched cathedral,
> Lay there, and ruins of great creatures else
> More like a shipwrecked fleet, too vast they seemed
> For all the life that is to animate:
> And vegetable rocks, tall sculptured palms,
> Pines grown, not hewn, in stone; and giant ferns,
> Whose earthquake-shaken leaves bore graves for nest.

Moreover, though his dramas are all but unreadable as wholes, his technical mastery of blank verse is remarkable, and he could also write lyrics matchless in design and melody, such as the lovely epithalamium from *Death's Jest Book*—

> *Female Voices*
>
> We have bathed, where none have seen us,
>> In the lake and in the fountain,
>> Underneath the charmed statue
> Of the timid, bending Venus,
>> When the water-nymphs were counting,
> In the waves the stars of night,
>> And those maidens started at you,
> Your limbs shone through so soft and bright.

But no secrets dare we tell,
    For thy slaves unlace thee,
    And he, who shall embrace thee,
Waits to try thy beauty's spell.

Male Voices

We have crowned thee queen of women,
    Since love's love, the rose, has kept her
Court within thy lips and blushes
    And thine eye, in beauty swimming,
Kissing, we rendered up the sceptre,
    At whose touch the startled soul
Like an ocean bounds and gushes,
    And spirits bend at thy control,
But no secrets dare we tell,
    For thy slaves unlace thee,
    And he, who shall embrace thee,
Is at hand, and so farewell.

The story of Beddoes's life gives us a picture as strange and unsatisfactory as his writings. He was born in 1803, the son of Thomas Beddoes, the celebrated physician. The latter was a sufficiently remarkable and forceful character. He was the intimate friend of Richard Lovell Edgeworth, Maria Edgeworth's father, and married his other daughter, Anna Maria Edgeworth, who became the poet's mother. Thomas Beddoes was a member of the brilliant, if somewhat eccentric Lichfield circle, which, besides the Edgeworths and himself, included Erasmus Darwin, Day (author of *Sandford and Merton*), and the poetess Anna Seward. The history of this group furnishes a noteworthy example of the kind of intellectual life which could flourish, in the eighteenth century, even in a provincial town such as Lichfield. They were the "left-wing intellectuals" of the day. Strongly influenced by the teachings of Rousseau, they were sympathetic to the ideals of the French Revolution, and developed theories, especially on the education of children, which were in many ways enlightened. At the same time they combined a taste for literature with an enthusiasm for experimental science. Thomas Beddoes was forced to resign his position as Reader in Chemistry at Oxford (where, it is worth noting, he asked the Bodleian Library to purchase books by German writers, including poets, philosophers and divines) on account of his revolutionary sympathies. He became one of the leading physicians of his day, and many of his ideas were in advance of his time. He interested himself in the medical use of gases, and founded the Pneumatic Institution. Sir Humphry Davy was his colleague.

The scientific and revolutionary interests of the elder Beddoes left their mark in the poetry of his son, who followed his father's profession. Beddoes drew upon scientific as well as romantic sources for his grotesque imagery. In the fragment already quoted on the subterranean city, for instance, we detect the influence of the palæontological researches which were being initiated by the work of Cuvier and others.

Beddoes went up to Pembroke College, Oxford, in 1820, but after taking his B.A. degree in 1825, left for Germany to study medicine at Göttingen. He studied under Blumenbach —who, among other things, was a pioneer of scientific ethnology, and possessed a famous collection of human skulls —and showed himself as a brilliant pupil, extremely keen on his medical studies. Benjamin Bernard Reich, a young Jew, the son of a banker in Podolia, became Beddoes's close friend at Göttingen. Reich translated Schiller into Hebrew, and Beddoes, who in 1827 began to share rooms with him, also learnt Hebrew, as well as Arabic. In 1829, however, he was sent down from Göttingen for drunkenness and riotous behaviour, but went with Reich to Würzburg, where he studied under Schonlein. Behr, a friend of Schonlein, was the leader of the Germania association of the Burschenschaftler, who aimed at a united Germany. Beddoes joined this revolutionary organization in 1831, being the only foreigner admitted to its membership, and contributed radical articles to the press. His political activities led to his expulsion from Würzburg by order of the Government in the following year. Henceforth it is not always easy to keep track of Beddoes's unsettled and somewhat irregular life in Germany and Switzerland. He wandered from town to town, returning only once or twice to England, and at long intervals. He occasionally practised as a doctor, and was involved in politics. In 1846 he met Konrad Degen, a good-looking young man of thirty-five, who followed his stepfather's trade as a baker, but whose ambition was to become an actor.[1] In 1847 they travelled together in Switzerland. But Degen having left him at Basle, Beddoes in a fit of melancholy depression, attempted suicide by severing an artery in his leg. While receiving medical attention he aggravated the wound by tearing off the bandages, and gangrene setting in, the limb had to be amputated. Though Degen subsequently returned to him, Beddoes appears never entirely to have recovered from the physical weakness and melancholy produced by this incident, and, in 1849, he took his own life by poison. "I am food for what I am good for—worms . . . I ought to have been, among a variety of other things, a good poet. Life was too great a bore on one peg, and that a bad one"—these are among the characteristic phrases of the brief note, addressed to one of his friends, found pinned upon his body.

A very strange man; yet there is a queer consistency about his life, as about his work, for which a psychological explanation should not be impossible. Beddoes's letters combine a faculty of acute comment on the life and literature of his time, a fantastic, self-tormenting humour, and a curious reserve. He is more sparing of expressions of affection for his friends than almost any other writer of the time. In his personal manner he is said to have been cynical and positively misanthropic; he describes himself as a "non-conductor of

---

[1] Degen had joined a touring company in 1837, but afterwards returned to his shop. He became a member of the Frankfurt Theatre in 1855, and acted, mostly in minor comic roles, till his retirement in 1878. He died in 1884.

friendship... a not-very-likeable person". Yet this character, the life-long duration of the few friendships he did make, the loyalty of Kelsall, his literary executor, the passages of an almost feminine tenderness which sometimes shine out amid the dark and cruel texture of his plays, belie. It seems to me a likely supposition that Beddoes was, in fact, always acutely aware of a homosexual temperament and proclivities. He was, at the same time, possessed of a powerful capacity for intellectual self-analysis and a strong emotional reserve. This would have checked and distorted his acute physical sensibilities, and deflected his passions, denied a normal outlet, towards the contemplation of death for its own sake.

To such a man the human body, image of his own physical limitations, would be an object at once fascinating and horrible; the means whereby, through the senses, he became cognizant of the universe, and a persistent clog and prison to the aspiring intellect. Such a hypothesis explains the continual juxtaposition of images of beauty with those of physical horror in Beddoes's poetry, and the remarkable manner in which his sensuous and intellectual perceptions are unified. This intellectual preoccupation with the physical may have been one of the subconscious motives which prompted him to the sudden decision of following his father's profession of medicine, instead of that of literature for which he had originally designed himself. This also may have made him so good an anatomist—the best pupil that Blumenbach ever had. His experiences in the dissecting room would only serve to enhance his innate sense of the fallibility and corruptibility of the human frame, and his consciousness of the skeleton which underlay all its beauty.

The study of medicine sent Beddoes to Germany. Yet before he had contemplated this career, he had already begun the study of the German language and literature—not a common accomplishment in those days. It was natural that a country which historical causes had ordained to be the fruitful soil of a metaphysical and quasi-mystical poetry of Death,

should make a powerful call to his nature. In the under-
ground revolutionary activities in which he engaged himself
there, we may suppose that he sought to sublimate his
frustrated cravings for human love and comradeship, together
with his inner sense of conflict with the settled order of
things.

In one, at least, of his German contemporaries, Beddoes
might have found a spiritual brother. The career of Georg
Büchner offers an extraordinary parallel to that of the English poet. Both men were students of medicine and of
anatomy, both were involved—Georg Büchner more closely
than Beddoes—in the German revolutionary movement of
the day, and both died before their time. In the writings of
both, too, we discover the same combination of cynicism and
a love of the grotesque, finding its expression in dramas
saturated with the imagery of death, whose immediate inspiration sprang from the English Elizabethans, yet which
nevertheless strike us to-day as extraordinarily modern in
their tone. Büchner, however, in spite of his having died at
the age of only twenty-four, appears to me to have possessed
the more virile and maturer genius. His world is not, like
that of Beddoes, one of pure fantasy. In his *Danton's Death*
the subject-matter—the great historical event of modern
Europe, the French Revolution—though projected into a
world of myth, has an urgency and a relevancy which
Beddoes's plays, set in imaginary and impossible Renaissance
courts, do not possess. And in his *Woyzek* there flashes
through the nightmare atmosphere a real humanity—a sense
of pity for the uneducated common man of modern civilization, baulked and tortured by a world whose complexities he
cannot either overcome or understand—which we look for
in vain in Beddoes.

In the work of Beddoes, as in that of many other homosexual writers, we detect an element of extreme subjectivism
—an inability to describe normal situations and emotions as
well as a quality of "unnaturalness" about the imagery.

These are the result of an imperfectly integrated personality and of the lack of a fully adult sense of the reality of the external world. Yet Beddoes's work is cast almost entirely in dramatic mould, and the drama is of all forms of art the most objective, and that requiring the firmest grip upon external realities. We are faced here with a contradiction, yet I think we may perhaps resolve it. We must suppose that Beddoes was aware—how far consciously or not it is difficult to say—of the limitations of his own subjective outlook, and sought, by adopting the dramatic form, to overcome it, and to externalize himself in characters which should seem to live in their own right. His letters show how justly he appreciated the problems which confronted those writers who sought to create a Romantic verse-drama in England:

> "Say what you will, I am convinced the man who is to awaken the drama must be a bold trampling fellow—no creeper into wormholes—no reviver, even, however good. These reanimations are vampire cold. Such ghosts as Marlowe, Webster, etc., are better dramatists, better poets, I dare say, than any contemporary of ours, but they are ghosts—the worm is in their pages,—and we want to see something that our great-grandsires did not know. With the greatest reverence for all the antiquities of the drama, I still think that we had better beget than revive, attempt to give the literature of this age an idiosyncrasy and spirit of its own, and only raise a ghost to gaze on not to live with. Just now the drama is a haunted ruin."

Yet despite the soundness of these remarks, Beddoes's plays, as plays, are failures. They are not easy reading, on the whole, even as closed dramas, and no one would dream of attempting to put them on the stage. They contain, I dare say, not one single character or situation to which the normal spectator could give his credence. Despite what he said in the passage quoted above, Beddoes merely succeeds in reviving the trappings of the later Elizabethan drama, wherewith to clothe the projections of his own inner and distorted vision.

That Beddoes was acutely conscious of his failure, his continual dissatisfaction with and rehandling of *Death's Jest Book*, his principal work, sufficiently proves. The deeper psychological disease of which it was a symptom, together with the sense of isolation which this, and his inevitable lack of sympathy with the general literary tendencies of his age, must have induced, led to his ever-growing expression of misanthropy, and to his fits of depression. That such a man, at forty-five already middle-aged, should have sought consolation in his friendship with Degen, whose aspirations to become an actor must have seemed to point towards the realization in another form of that dramatic reality which Beddoes had learned to revere in the Elizabethans, and pursued so long in vain in his own work, is understandable. There is something very touching in the story that Beddoes, newly arrived in Zurich, chartered the town theatre for the night in order to give his friend an opportunity of playing Hotspur. That the relationship should have ended tragically was perhaps also natural.

The Romantic Movement is capable of several, and in some degree contradictory, interpretations. From one aspect it may be said to have found its voice at the prospect of that triumph of reason and human progress for which the French Revolution seemed to be the signal. But from another it may be regarded as a reaction against the growing scientific empiricism of the age, thence expressing itself in a rediscovery of the culture of the Middle Ages, and a reaffirmation of spiritual values as against those of merely material progress. But while the spiritual view of the nature of the universe which the Middle Ages enjoyed had its basis in an intellectual system of philosophy generally accepted throughout Christendom, for the nineteenth-century Romantics the task of discovering spiritual realities devolved upon the subjective imaginative intuitions of individuals. The poets, lacking an adequate metaphysic upon which to erect their vision of things, had to construct their own personal "philosophies"

from the data provided by direct and intense emotional experience. The strain, spiritual and moral, produced by the
continual pursuit of these experiences was inevitably very
great. The incomplete character of the life-works of Wordsworth and Coleridge, the early deaths of Byron, Shelley, and
Keats, may have been due in part to the inability of these
poets to stand this strain. Moreover, the intense and rapid
exploration of so much emotional experience involved the
swift passage, in the course of three generations, from the
world of exalted feelings in which Wordsworth's poetry has
its existence, to the region of eccentric fantasy in which the
poets considered in this chapter are at home. If in the work of
Beddoes imaginative experience leads us into tracts of feeling
strange to the normal healthy mind, in a few poems of
Thomas Hood we reach a state of spiritual disorganization,
exhaustion, and decay which marks one limit of that continent of the imagination mapped out by Romantic poetry.

Thomas Hood died on May 3rd, 1845, being then aged not
quite forty-six years. He did not do so in easy circumstances;
his life, indeed, had been one long struggle against poverty,
as well as disease. Yet his death could not pass unnoted—like
the obscure suicide of Beddoes in Basle four years later. The
hard-working journalist and public jester might be called one
of the best-known and most popular literary figures of the
day. In due course a monument was erected, by public
subscription, over his grave in Kensal Green cemetery.

Attics and lumber-rooms and the shelves of second-hand
bookshops bear witness to his popularity, which lasted
throughout the Victorian era: edition upon cheap edition of
the *Poems*, the *Humorous Poems*, of selections, in the peculiarly
hideous bindings of the period. Even in my own first school-
days, in the late nineteen-twenties, we were still brought up
on *Eugene Aram*, which, like the no less popular *Song of the
Shirt* and *Bridge of Sighs*, moves in that gas-lit, fuggy world of
sentimental pity and melodramatic terror which characterizes the contemporaneous novels of Dickens. But it was as a

4

writer of humorous verse that Hood was most esteemed. Even Professor Oliver Elton in his *The English Muse* summarizes him as "that pleasant bard 'of passion and of mirth'", and an early editor and anthologist, prefacing a selection of his poems, couples his name with that of Praed.

Few comparisons, it seems to me, could be more inept. The exquisite, smiling, aristocratic Praed, with his perfect command of raillery—the last glitter of the courtly raillery of the seventeenth and eighteenth centuries—carries a poet's sensitiveness into the empty, pompous world of high Whig and Tory politics of the reign of William IV. There is a wistfulness behind his smile, but he does not allow it to break through the smooth surface of his art. Though he is Hood's contemporary, he belongs spiritually to another century. Hood, like Keats, is of the still half-submerged lower middle class. He is in everything a poet of transition. He stands midway between the storm and stress of the Romantics and the spiritual uncertainties of the Victorian poets; unevenness and bad taste everywhere give evidence of an inner struggle behind his work.

I doubt if any sensitive person can now read Hood's humorous verse with much pleasure. It was with his *tours de force* as a punster that he delighted his original readers. We are struck at once by the contrast between this nineteenth-century facetiousness and the comic, or tragic, punning of the Elizabethans. In the latter there is the exuberance of the discoverer, the inventor. The poets are exploring the new potentialities of language, the hidden relations between things and ideas revealed by the accidental similarities in the sound of words. In Hood we are only conscious of a fevered desire to torture the maximum of purely mechanical entertainment out of them. The puns come at us in a regular barrage, emphasized by the tick-tock rhythms, parodying the manner of the broadsheet street ballad, but the imagination is not called upon to play its part. Even the densest and least-educated reader of *Hood's Own* cannot possibly miss the

witticism. There is the weariness of the literary drudge behind these verses. Their subjects are, in fact, often painful.
Frustrated spinsters, deserted maidens, ghosts, cannibalism
(on which pleasant topic both Gilbert and Thackeray were
later to be excruciatingly funny), became stock themes for
Victorian wit. And this sort of thing, I believe, came in with
the frayed nerves of Tom Hood. The little illustrations,
rather horridly grotesque, which embellish the original
Annuals, go with the verses all too well. Hood was the victim
of his age, but had he really possessed a comic genius, he
might have been its tragic fool; as it is, except in *The Last
Man*, he is only a sad one.

Sometimes, indeed, Hood attempted to retaliate: *Miss
Kilmansegg*, a burlesque directed against the now-dominant
class of Philistine plutocrats. But it is too gentle to be effective.
The famous *Bridge of Sighs* and *Song of the Shirt* show, if we
could not discover it from his life, that Hood's heart was in
the right place, though it seems to me that they have neither
strength of style nor adequate social insight to justify the
very high praise that has sometimes been given them. *Eugene
Aram* is melodrama, and good melodrama, but second-rate
poetry. It is, however, in his poems of a more sombre
colouring—such as the *Ode to Autumn*, and his exercises in
the macabre—*The Last Man*, *The Haunted House*, and *Lycus
the Centaur*—that Hood's imagination enters upon a world
which is characteristically its own.

It was, however, only after these early serious Romantic
poems, which included *The Two Swans*, *The Plea of the Midsummer Fairies*, the *Ode to Autumn*, and *Lycus the Centaur*,
had failed to attract much attention from the general
reading public, that Hood turned to comic writing. The year
1821, in which he was introduced into the liberal and literary
circle of which Leigh Hunt was the centre, may be reckoned
as decisive in his poetic development. He made the acquaintance of Lamb, Hazlitt, and De Quincey, and, above all, of
John Hamilton Reynolds. For this year Keats had died at

Rome, and it was through the latter friend that something of the authentic spirit of Keats himself was transmitted to Hood's own poetry. That poetry has all the occasional faults which characterized the "Cockney School", and into which Keats himself too frequently lapsed—the floridity, the over-sweetness, the touches of vulgarity of sentiment. But when he rids his style of these blemishes Hood shows himself in the direct line of the Romantic tradition, and is far from the second-rateness, as of something machine-made, which was to mark so much of Tennyson's polished Victorian resumption of the Keatsian style.

The world of Keats had been a world of sensuous richness, full to the point of being over-ripe. Keats himself, as he matured in experience, had begun to realize how easily that world might dissolve at the touch of disenchantment, and that progress is envisaged in *La Belle Dame Sans Merci* and the conclusion of *Lamia*. In Hood's poetry we indeed wake "on the cold hill-side". Even in the somewhat pretty-pretty *Plea of the Midsummer Fairies* it is the dark figure of destroying Time which dominates the scene.

The sonnet on *Silence* well defines the nature of Hood's peculiar territory of feeling:

> There is a silence where hath been no sound,
>   There is a silence where no sound may be,
>   In the cold grave—under the deep, deep sea,
> Or in wide desert, where no life is found,
> Which hath been mute, and still must sleep profound;
>   No voice is hushed, no life treads silently,
>   But clouds and cloudy shadows wander free,
> That never spoke, over the idle ground;
>   But in green ruins, in the desolate walls
> Of antique palaces, where man hath been
>   Though the dun fox, or wild hyena, calls
> And owls that flit continually between,
>   Quick to the echo, and the low winds moan,
>   There the true silence is, self-conscious and alone.

It is a world where life *has been*, where things have been held together in a consistent order of love and beauty, but which is now only filled with images of physical death and decay, and intellectual and emotional contradiction. *The Haunted House* owes its whole effectiveness to the skilful piling up of such images. It is significant that when the climax of the poem is reached, the ghost which appears is a daylight ghost. This not only intensifies the strangeness of the poem, but suggests also, perhaps, that the image of terror which had begun to haunt the poetry of the later Romantics, is now no longer confined to the night-side of thought, but has power to walk in the waking consciousness.

The subject of *The Last Man* had a peculiar appeal to the Romantic poets, which is not difficult to explain. It was treated by Campbell, by Byron, by Beddoes, and by Mrs. Shelley, but Hood's poem is much the most successful handling of the theme. The hero of the poem finds himself almost the sole survivor in a world whose inhabitants have been extermi-nated by a great plague. In form especially, as well as to some extent in subject, the poem has a closer affinity to Coleridge's *Ancient Mariner* than any other in English. But here there is no redemption; in this world even natural human affection is dead. The only companion which the hero finds, a beggar, he hangs upon the gallows, and is left in complete loneliness, except for the savage animals which threaten his life. He is afraid even to hang himself on the same gallows—

> For there is not another man alive,
> In the world, to pull my legs!

The fantastic horror of this poem is enhanced by the detailed actuality of its description, a trait very characteristic of Hood's work at its best.

It is very profitable to compare Hood's *Ode to Autumn* with Keats's poem on the same subject, from which, and from the *Ode on Melancholy*, it largely derives. Keats's *Autumn* is full of a sense of physical and spiritual well-being and completeness. It is the "mellow fruitfulness" of the season that is emphasized throughout; there is no sadness as the poet contemplates the dying year. Keats was staying at Winchester, and thus describes the weather which inspired the poem:

"How beautiful the season is now—How fine the air. A temperate sharpness about it. Really, without joking, chaste weather—Dian skies—I never lik'd stubble-fields so much as now—Aye better than the chilly green of the Spring. Somehow a stubble-plain looks warm—this struck me so much in my Sunday's walk that I composed upon it."

In Hood's poem, on the contrary, it is always the sadness and decay of autumn which are underlined. The poem has not the rounded, satisfying quality of Keats's *Ode*, but it possesses a wild, melancholy music of its own, and does not lose by comparison. There is one curious inconsistency in its design. In the opening stanza autumn is personified as an old man, but at the close of the poem as a female figure. The first stanza is also markedly shorter, and different in its metrical build to the others. I would hazard a guess that it was composed first, and the fragment laid aside for some time; and that Hood wrote the remainder of the poem at one sitting, under the pressure of strong emotion, not altogether consciously realized. This would not only explain the inconsistency noted above, but also the strong, compelling, fluid rhythm of the later stanzas, which sweep on to the end with hardly a break in the sense, and also the peculiar emotional intensity of the poem. The melancholy and terror conveyed by much of the imagery are in excess of the actual emotions which would be excited by the theme of autumn, considered purely as the death of summer and the passage of the year into a season of cold and darkness. It is an autumn of the Spirit that is described in the closing lines:

O go and sit with her, and be o'ershaded
Under the languid downfall of her hair:
She wears a coronal of flowers faded
Upon her forehead, and a face of care;

There is enough of withered everywhere
To make her bower,—and enough of gloom;
There is enough of sadness to invite,
If only for the rose that died—whose doom
Is beauty's,—she that with the living bloom
Of conscious cheeks most beautifies the light;
There is enough of sorrowing, and quite
Enough of chilly droppings from her bowl,
Enough of fear and shadowy despair,
To frame her cloudy prison for the soul!

For what have fear and shadowy despair to do with the mere temporal passage of the seasons? Again in the lines:

Where are the merry birds?—away, away,
On panting wings through the inclement skies,
Lest owls should prey
Undazzled at noon-day
And tear with horny beak their lustrous eyes,

there is a sudden stab of physical pain and horror in the last image, which startles and shocks us. Yet it is known that Hood was the kindest and gentlest of men. It is his own familiarity with pain, both bodily and mental, which forces this cry from him.

Lycus the Centaur is one of the most extraordinary of Hood's fantastic poems, written in a jolting, anapæstic metre which serves to emphasize the wildness and terror of the theme. It is a short mythological narrative. Lycus finds himself in the magic dominion of Circe, whose love he has refused. It is haunted by animals and filled with plants which have been transformed by her sorceries. He meets and loves the water nymph Aegle. She tries to obtain a charm which will render him immortal, but Circe instead gives her an incantation which is to turn her lover into a horse; perceiving its effect, Aegle breaks off in the middle, and Lycus is left a centaur and flees away, to spend the rest of his existence in

isolation from the haunts of men, whose love and companionship he longs for in vain.

The poem is a vision of the world as it must have appeared
to Hood's imagination, tormented by disease, exposed to the
cruel pressure of a hostile world. A sense of pitiful frustration pervades the story; love is everywhere divorced from its
proper mode of operation. The victims of Circe's magic
approach Lycus with motions of affection and gentleness.
But their animal forms appal him.

> They were mournfully gentle, and grouped for relief,
> All foes in their skin, but all friends in their grief;
> The leopard was there,—baby-mild in its feature;
> And the tiger, black-barred, with the gaze of a creature
> That knew gentle pity; the bristle backed boar,
> His innocent tusks stained with mulberry-gore;
> And the laughing Hyena, but laughing no more;
> And the snake, not with magical orbs to devise
> Strange death, but with woman's attraction of eyes;
> The tall ugly ape, that still bore a dim shine
> Through his hairy eclipse of a manhood divine;
>
> .   .   .
>
> There were woes of all shapes, wretched forms, when I came,
> That hung down their heads with a human-like shame;
> The elephant hid in the boughs, and the bear
> Shed over his eyes the dark veil of his hair;
> And the womanly soul turning sick with disgust,
> Tried to vomit herself from her serpentine crust;
> While all groaned their groans into one at their lot,
> As I brought them the image of what they were not.

The reader may be significantly reminded of H. G. Wells's
story of *The Island of Dr. Moreau,* a nightmare of the spirit
of man imprisoned in an inhuman universe of the scientific
intellect. But there is a profounder parallel with an earlier
and immeasurably greater imaginative vision. The grief of

Lycus is like the grief of Dante when he beholds the human form pitifully distorted in the bodies of some of the damned. There is another passage still more infernal:

> For once, at my suppering, I plucked in the dusk
> An apple, juice-gushing, and fragrant of musk;
> But by daylight my fingers were crimsoned with gore
> And the half-eaten fragment was flesh at the core;
> And once—only once—for the love of its blush,
> I broke a broom-bough, but there came such a gush
> On my hand, that I fainted away in weak fright.

Here we have a far-off echo of the Wood of the Suicides, in the thirteenth canto of the *Inferno*. Lycus becomes aware of sorrowful female forms, images of temptation, or his own impotent pity. They try to seize him with hands "blood-stained of the breast they had mangled" but he flees them, his soul already filled with an animal fear. In this half-realized hell of disintegration the nymph Aegle, rising from the still pool of contemplation, comes as a vehicle of love which promises redemption. But at the moment their love is to be consummated and immortality gained for Lycus, it is Circe, the image of brutalizing lust, who appears in Aegle's shape. All that the love of the water-nymph is able to accomplish is to save Lycus from complete transformation into an animal; and the partly human shape he retains, renders him only the more acutely conscious of his degradation.

The last action of the poem is a pathetic picture of a soul which longs for affection, and finds only hostility. Lycus encounters a child—here surely another image of love is offered him:

> He came; with his face of bold wonder, to feel
> The hair of my side, and to lift up my heel,
> And questioned my face with wide eyes; but when under
> My lids he saw tears,—for I wept at his wonder,
> He stroked me, and uttered such kindliness then,
> That the once love of women, the friendship of men

In past sorrow, no kindness e'er came like a kiss
In my heart in its desolate day such as this!
And I yearned at his cheeks in my love, and down bent,
And lifted him up in my arms with intent
To kiss him,—but he cruel-kindly, alas!
Held out to my lips a plucked handful of grass!
Then I dropt him in horror, but felt as I fled
The stone he indignantly hurled at my head.

It is made clear in the poem that this boy is the infant
Hercules, destined at last to be the destroyer of the whole
race of centaurs whom Lycus now goes to seek as his only and
inevitable companions. The Hero, intended as a Saviour-
figure for mankind, can only appear as the stern Destroyer
for the soul rendered monstrous by sin.

In Hood's poetry, as in Beddoes's, and to a less extent in
Darley's, on the threshold of the Victorian era, the Terrible
is seen in process of disintegrating into the Horrible. The
tragic view of life gives way to the melodramatic, as, in
another sphere, the comic-sublime degenerates into mere
facetiousness. I should distinguish the Terrible and the
Horrible in poetry as follows: in Dante, in the tragedies of
Shakespeare, to some degree in all truly great and serious art,
we are inevitably presented, along with the other elements
which go to make up human experience, with images of pain,
suffering, and death, spiritual as well as bodily; of distortions
of the soul, and perversions of beauty. Such images we call
"terrible"; but it is only a spiritual cowardice which shrinks
from their contemplation, and in experiencing the imaginative work of the great masters, we are conscious that however terrible, at times, the vision, the imagination which has
called it forth, also comprehends it intellectually; in the
lowest pit of Hell, Dante still knows Virgil, the inherited
tradition of the human intellect, at his side as guide, pro-
tector, and interpreter.

The Horrible in art, on the other hand, meets us when the
intellectual power of co-ordination in the artist is no longer

adequate to his imaginative and emotional perceptions. Evil, embodying itself in symbols and figures of physical ugliness and fear, is seen as it were in flashes, lurking in dark corners. But its nature is not comprehended; it is not intellectually co-ordinated with the great images of beauty and love.

After the first visions of the Romantics faded, the Victorian Age failed to find a philosophy sufficiently universal in scope, whereby the nature of evil might be envisaged. Nor can the Englishman of the period be pronounced guiltless of a deliberate refusal to face the fact of evil in the universe. A facile optimism and belief in the inevitability of progress too often went hand in hand with a failure to recognize, on the one side, the nature of the social and economic abuses arising out of industrial capitalism, on the other, of the whole complicated problem of sex. The age of acute sexual repression in ordinary social life, saw, in literature, among other things, the development of the ghost story as a fine art form. The works of Wilkie Collins, Mrs. Oliphant and others—above all Sheridan Le Fanu (many of whose tales, such as *Green Tea*, could quite easily be restated, in the light of modern analysis, in terms of neurotic psychology)—achieve a subtlety of atmosphere, which renders them as far superior to the productions of the Gothic amateurs of the eighteenth century, as they are to those of their few modern successors. This horror is a reflex of lust operating in the subconscious world of dream and death-imagery and of social fear. In the poetry of Browning and Tennyson the element of the Horrible persists, though it peeps out obscenely, and for brief moments only, from amid the gilded decoration of Tennyson's verse, and Browning's tortuous thickets of half-digested thought. Browning indeed, though he possesses a less restricted and more vigorous fancy (and far less of purely poetic sensibility), has a distant affinity to Beddoes. He was capable, in *Childe Roland*, of a pure exercise in the Horrible. It is to be noted that, for all its masterly handling of atmosphere, the emphasis

in this poem is not on moral evil, but on sheer physical pain
and beastliness:

> —Good saints, how I feared
> To set my foot upon a dead man's cheek,
> Each step, or feel the spear I thrust to seek
> For hollows, tangled in his hair or beard!
> It may have been a water-rat I speared,
> But ugh! it sounded like a baby's shriek.

So also in *The Heretic's Tragedy*, despite its profounder
subject. But usually the horror is felt only as a momentary
shudder—arising, for instance, from such an image as the
"lump of lapis lazuli. . . . Big as a Jew's head cut off at the
nape" of *The Bishop Orders his Tomb*—such images have
nothing to do with the intellectual creed of courage and
optimism which was the outward face Browning turned to
the world.

In Tennyson the horror is of less physical and greater
emotional intensity. It arises from his sense of loneliness,
frustration, and despair; imaged by the wind that "shrills all
night in a waste land, where no one comes, or hath come since
the making of the world"—over the bleak flats of Lincolnshire, his childhood's home, which give such an air of dreari-
ness to *Mariana* and *The Passing of Arthur*. Tennyson has
dreamt of the obscene thing, the Kraken, lurking in the
subconscious depths of the mind; his soul, imprisoned in its
own Palace of Art becomes aware of this devil:

> But in dark corners of her palace stood
>   Uncertain shapes; and unawares
> On white-eyed phantasms weeping tears of blood,
>   And horrible nightmares,
>
> And hollow shades enclosing hearts of flame,
>   And with dim-fretted foreheads all,
> On corpses three months old at noon she came,
>   That stood against the wall.

But the poet is unable to resolve these images, and the "moral" of the poem is trite and commonplace. It is not until we reach what have often indeed been termed the "terrible" sonnets of Gerard Manley Hopkins, that English poetry recovers enough intellectual intensity to envisage evil, not in moments of waking nightmare, but in its naked reality.

Chapter 2

THE REGIONALISTS—THE END OF A TRADITION

THERE is in English poetry, as in that of all other nations, a tradition of the folk, which lies behind, and is always influencing the great literary tradition. It manifests itself in May-day carol and harvest-song, in children's rhymes and dance-games, in ballads, humorous or moralizing—which often find their way into printed broadsheets—in certain hymns and spontaneous expressions of piety, and, lastly, traditions, in the rhymed epitaph. This folk-poetry has its roots in the old-fashioned village community, with its traditional occupations, and its seasonal rhythm of occasional holidays and festivals. Many of the songs are designed primarily to accompany and facilitate labour. They are thus bound up with the cottage crafts and industries. In such a community, the sedentary occupations, such as spinning, are primarily the province of women; that is why, in genuine folk-song, the burden of the emotion so often lies upon the heroine, who is commonly the speaker in the love-songs and in many ballads. This pattern of life the agrarian revolution, with its enclosure system, which enriched the well-to-do farmers while it deprived the smaller peasants of the common lands on which their livelihood largely depended, destroyed. At the same time, the industrial revolution brought to an end the traditional cottage industries. All through the nineteenth century the traditional way of life in the English village was a thing dying or already dead. At the beginning of that era, collectors began to take notice of the words of these folk-songs; the music was to be recovered somewhat later as a result of the labours of Cecil Sharp and others. It was almost too late.

We must not suppose this song-making of the village to be

a tradition altogether unlearned or anonymous. In the moral carols and ballads, in particular, we sometimes note the hand of the curate or the village schoolmaster. In the village community of the earlier centuries, it was often their education alone, and not their income or fundamental way of life, which differentiated such men from most of their neighbours. Besides the professional ballad-singer, adapting for his songs formulas and plots inherited from the mediæval minstrel, there were also poets among the peasantry themselves who made songs from their own experiences, or from some local jest or tradition. The beautiful song called *The Seeds of Love*, one of the more widely current of English folk-songs, is stated, in Bell's *Ballads and Songs of the Peasantry of England* (1862), to have been composed by a Mrs. Fleetwood Habergham, who died in 1703. It is her lament for her unhappy marriage, and is interesting as showing how the folk-poet quite naturally made use of a conventional symbolism to figure her emotions.

I sowed the seeds of love, it was all in the Spring
In April, May, and June, likewise, when small birds they do sing;
My garden's well-planted with flowers everywhere,
Yet I had not the liberty to choose for myself the flower that I loved
   so dear.

My gardener he stood by, I asked him to choose for me,
He chose the violet, the lily and pink, and those I refused all three;
The violet I forsook, because it fades so soon,
The lily and the pink I did overlook, and I vowed I'd stay till June.

In June there's a red rose-bud, and that's the flower for me!
But often have I plucked at the red rose-bud till I gained the willow-
   tree;
The willow-tree will twist, and the willow-tree will twine,—
O! I wish I was in the dear youth's arms that once had the heart of mine.

My gardener he stood by, he told me to take great care,
For in the middle of a red rose-bud there grows a sharp thorn there;
I told him I'd take no care till I did feel the smart,
And often I plucked at the red rose-bud till I pierced it to the heart.

I'll make me a posy of hyssop,—no other I can touch,—
That all the world may plainly see I love one flower too much
My garden is run wild! where shall I plant a new—
For my bed, that once was covered with thyme, is all over run
  with rue.

There is an interchange, too, between the world of folk-
song and the literary world of the town. A glance at any
collection of broad-sheets will reveal, along with ballads which
obviously go back, in some cases, to originals as early as the
sixteenth century, songs by such writers as Burns, Moore, and
"Monk" Lewis, as well as snatches from eighteenth-century
glees and ballad operas. By such channels this literary material
gained an oral currency, even among the illiterate. It was
absorbed, as it were, into the stream of folk-tradition, and
was often curiously modified in the process. In one of the
English Mumming Plays edited by Professor Chambers,
which was still performed by a troupe of village Mummers
down to the present century, St. George and his companions
burst into a song, which proves, on investigation, to be a
garbled version of an aria from Addison's extremely artificial
and Italianate opera *Rosamund*.

These country songs, falling upon our ears to-day, call
forth feelings of nostalgia. The world in which they had
their birth is gone, and can never return. Yet, as long as it
existed, it remained a way of life in which values were still
fixed, and modes of thought and feeling had behind them the
backing of a long, historical tradition. And amid the intellectual and moral confusion of the nineteenth century, there
were certain poets who, by birth or by occupation, stood
close to this tradition, and whose technique is to a large
extent a development of that which they inherited from
their peasant neighbours and forefathers. In the early part of
the century, we have not only Clare, who sprang directly
from the peasant class, but also William Barnes and Robert
Stephen Hawker, village priests from the west country who
participated sufficiently closely in the life of the communities

of farmers and labourers among whom they lived, for their work to have, for all their scholarship and relative sophistication, something of the essential qualities of the folk-tradition. In a later generation the same tradition is continued, though with a more self-conscious and intellectual attitude, in the poetry of Thomas Hardy. In the work of these poets, it seems to me, there is a soundness scarcely to be found in that of their more polite contemporaries.

John Clare is the only notable English (as distinct from Scottish) poet to have sprung directly from the ranks of the agricultural workers. (Hogg, the "Ettrick Shepherd" must be classed as a Scottish poet, though he was actually born a little south of the Border.) Moreover, it must be remembered that for considerable periods of his life, he himself worked on the land. There is a peculiar poignancy in the story of this Northamptonshire villager whose genius was discovered by well-meaning literary patrons; who was unable, afterwards, either to fit contentedly again into the world of the peasantry from which he had been taken, or to find a secure position in any other sphere; of his confinement as a madman, and his death, so many years afterwards, solitary and almost forgotten, in that condition. It might indeed have been expected. Things of the same sort had happened before. There had been, as long ago as the time of George II and his Queen Caroline, the unfortunate Stephen Duck, by origin a day-labourer, who received the patronage of the Queen, and who also died mad. There had been, a few years before Clare's time, Robert Bloomfield, another ill-starred poet, whose *The Farmer's Boy* nevertheless achieved a popularity which continued even when Clare's infinitely superior poems were ignored. Bloomfield's talents were but slight, and seem quickly to have been smothered under the literary eighteenth-century manner which he acquired, and which he practised after a competent, but somewhat featureless fashion. The unlucky history of Burns, a more vigorous, though not a more inspired poet than Clare, comes to mind likewise. Yet the

5

strange fate of Clare's poetry, the indifferent attitude taken up even by many of those who knew it, for generations after his death, is hard to explain. Only in this century have critics and scholars (above all, Edmund Blunden and E. W. and A. Tibble) really begun to realize its merits and bring them before the generality of readers. Yet Clare must be treated as occupying a peculiar, though not necessarily a minor place in the hierarchy of the Romantic poets; no longer merely as a curiosity.

John Clare was born in 1793 at Helpston, a village near Peterborough. His father, Parker Clare, was the illegitimate son of John Donald Parker, a Scotsman, who had been the village schoolmaster. His mother was illiterate, but it is recorded that his father, who had an exceptional memory, had a stock of more than a hundred ballads which he could repeat by heart. Clare is also said to have learned a number of such songs from an old woman, known as Granny Bains, herself illiterate, in his native village.

Clare was sent to a village dame's school, and later, between the ages of seven and twelve, attended a day-school at Glinton. In order to obtain the money which made this possible, he helped his father with threshing and other work. The books which Clare read in his early boyhood give a fair idea of the kind of literary culture which was current amongst the peasantry, and which fertilized, so to speak, the folk-tradition. Besides the Bible and Prayer Book, they included *Robinson Crusoe*, and a number of sixpenny chap-book romances and penny broad-sheet ballads, such as were brought to the village and to local fairs by the agency of pedlars and hawkers. Among these penny ballads was Wordsworth's *We are Seven*—this fact is a good illustration of the interchange between literary and folk-culture of which I have spoken. From an early age, too, he was familiar with the story of Chatterton, which formed the subject of a series of wood-cuts printed on a handkerchief—evidently a "fairing"—or bought from some itinerant pedlar. When Clare's father became crippled by rheumatism, Clare began working for neighbouring farmers in order to support him, at the same time attending a night-school at Glinton.

He had already begun to show himself of more than usual intelligence, and of a somewhat abnormal nervous sensibility. He began to be taken with "fits" every spring and autumn—and one cannot help suspecting that in these some kind of nervous disorder of a cyclic nature, the germ of his later insanity, was beginning to show itself. Clare himself attributed their occurrence to the shock induced by seeing a man break his neck by accidentally falling from a wagon. "The ghastly paleness of death", he wrote later of this incident, "struck such a terror on me that I could not forget it for years, and my dreams were constantly wandering in church-yards, digging graves, seeing spirits in charnel-houses, etc."

The reading of Thomson's *Seasons* first prompted Clare to try his hand at verse-making. He was at first too shy to acknowledge his poems as his own, but the praise which they received from friends encouraged him to continue. Soon, too, he fell in love with Mary Joyce, the daughter of a neighbouring farmer. Clare had no prospects, and the girl's father would not permit them to get married. Clare saw her for the last time in 1816, but this passionate, frustrated love was never to be forgotten—even after his marriage to Martha ("Patty") Turner in 1820. To Clare, Mary Joyce was always his "first wife", and later, in his madness, her figure was to reappear in his poetry, to the exclusion of that of Patty. Nor did he fail to note the symbolism of the two names, Mary and Martha —the ideal and the workaday reality.

Helpston had been largely farmed under the old open-field system, but in 1809 an Act was passed enclosing common lands there. This, which was for the benefit of the land-owners and richer farmers, was disastrous for the labourers, who thereby lost their strips of land on the common, and the chance of keeping a cow of their own. It was in the atmo-sphere of the disruption of the old community life, with a consequent loosening of morals and a decline in self-respect among individuals, that Clare grew up. Settled employment was not always easy to get. Clare worked as apprentice to a gardener on the Marquis of Exeter's estate for a short time, and during the Napoleonic wars served in the militia. From 1814 to 1817 he did gardening and other casual work on the land. At the same time he continued to read in the English poets (of whom he gradually amassed a library of his own) and to write prolifically. By a fortunate series of chances his poems were brought to the knowledge of John Taylor, Keats's publisher, who undertook to issue a volume of Clare's work. This book appeared in 1820, and was immediately a success. It received favourable review in the London press, and Clare gained some friends and patrons both among the local gentry and in London. He made several visits to the capital, where he met some of the literary figures of the day, including Lamb and Hood. Another of his acquaintances was Darley, with whom he corresponded, and whose example he followed in writing poems in imitation of the English seventeenth-century poets. Efforts were made on the part of various patrons to help Clare financially. A subscription list was opened for him, which provided him with a fixed income of a little more than forty pounds a year. This was about ten pounds more than he could have earned as a labourer, but he had his parents and a large family to support. Casual work on the land, with which he might have augmented his resources, was not, excepting during harvest-time, readily obtainable. His patrons were willing to assist him as a peasant-poet—a kind of curiosity. But that Clare should be given enough money to allow him to come permanently to London, and become a professional writer—that was unthinkable. Moreover, they were not always pleased by the "ungrateful" and "radical" sentiments which he occasionally expressed.

Clare's income was paid through Taylor, the publisher, who was, however, extremely unbusinesslike. When, in 1825,

Taylor's firm was dissolved, Clare found himself unexpectedly burdened with debt. For the next ten years, in spite of occasional assistance from patrons, Clare's financial worries continued. Neither of his later volumes of verse achieved the success of his first. Though they received favourable notice from the critics, the public would not buy them. Partly for economic reasons, the slump in poetry, which also affected Beddoes, Darley, and Hood, was operating here also. Moreover, his publishers allowed too long an interval to elapse between the appearance of each of his volumes, so that his name was not kept sufficiently before the public eye. Clare became increasingly nervous and ill. He seems to have suffered from delusions of persecution, and believed himself to be the victim of witchcraft. His behaviour began to grow eccentric. In 1837, his landlord and patron, Earl Fitzwilliam, proposed that he should be confined in a public lunatic asylum; but Taylor and other friends managed to save him from this, and to place him instead in a private institution at High Beech, in Epping Forest. Here he seems to have been well treated, Dr. Allen, the proprietor, being one of the most enlightened alienists of the day. The hallucinations from which he suffered at this period have been recorded. He believed himself to be married to Mary Joyce, while he was to describe Patty as "one of my fancies". He is also said to have given way to delusions that he was of noble descent— or, alternatively, that he was a prizefighter, and by offering to meet all comers, could raise the money he needed to pay off his debts.

In 1841, Clare escaped, and returned on foot to his Northamptonshire home, partly keeping himself alive by eating grass, which he picked by the roadside. His wife Patty looked after him, though he scarcely seemed to acknowledge her, still believing himself to be married to Mary, whom he called "Mary Clare". To her he addressed an extraordinarily interesting and poignant document, in which he gave an account of his journey home, after his escape from High

Beech. Patty did her best to prevent his being put away once more in an asylum. Nevertheless, in December 1841, he was certified as insane—because, among other things, it was alleged that he had been "years addicted to poetical prosing", and he was confined in the Northampton General Lunatic Asylum. Here he remained for another twenty-three years, almost forgotten by the world. Though his children came to visit him occasionally, Patty was too hard-worked and too poor to make the journey to Northampton. But he was kindly treated, and allowed a certain amount of liberty.

He continued to write, and to this period belong many of his most beautiful poems. Many of these are love songs, in which the idealized figure of Mary Joyce, whom he believed to be his wife, and the mother of a family of children by him, continually appears. He died in 1863, and was buried in the churchyard of his native village.

There is no need to sentimentalize Clare. From his portrait there looks out upon us a face of peculiar spiritual beauty. There is the disconcerting clarity of a child's gaze in those eyes, and a like quality in the expression of the sensitive mouth. Yet it is not a face softened by weakness, or intellectual and emotional immaturity. Clare's genius was great enough to bring itself to fruition, despite his social and economic disadvantages, and the difficulty of acquiring an education these entailed. But his nature was of a sort which inevitably doomed him to spiritual solitude; and this the accident of his birth served greatly to exacerbate. His best-known poem, written in Northampton Asylum, is justly famous as an expression of this loneliness:

> I am; but what I am, who cares, or knows,
>   My friends forsake me, like a memory lost;
> I am the self-consumer of my woes,
>   They rise and vanish, an oblivious host,
> Like shades in love, and Death's oblivion lost;
> And yet I am, and live with shadows tost

Into the nothingness of scorn and noise,
    Into the living sea of waking dreams,
Where there is neither sense of life nor joys,
    But the vast shipwreck of my life's esteems;
And e'en the dearest—that I loved the best—
Are strange—nay rather stranger than the rest.

I long for scenes where man has never trod—
    For scenes where woman never smiled or wept;
There to abide with my Creator, God,
    And deep as I in childhood sweetly slept;
Untroubling and untroubled where I lie;
The grass below—above the vaulted sky.

There is no self-pity in these lines, no reproach to the
world. The poet's loneliness is stated, the emotions arising
from it are not dwelt upon. Nor is there any craving for the
love and companionship that have been lost and can never be
regained, but desire rather for the peace of a greater solitude,
which is with God.

The badger, in Clare's own poem, with his stubbornness
and solitary courage, might be taken as a type of this poet, as
well as the lost "child-man" which some critics have presented to us:

He turns agen and drives the noisy crowd
And beats the many dogs in noises loud.
He drives away and beats them every one,
And then they loose them all and set them on,
Then starts and grins and drives the crowd agen;
Till kicked and torn and beaten out he lies
And leaves his hold, and cackles, groans and dies.

Clare's distinctive qualities as a poet are a peculiar sensitiveness and accuracy of observation, an unforced simplicity
of language, and an extreme integrity and purity of feeling.
The bulk of what he wrote is large. We find these qualities
generally diffused throughout his poetry, though somewhat

rarely attaining sufficient intensity to take hold upon the memory and imagination. Nevertheless, the general level of his work is remarkably high, and there is scarcely anything he wrote which does not show some touches of poetic feeling of a kind hardly any other poet can display. In the work of his early and middle periods we see him in full enjoyment of his new-found genius, experimenting and writing for the mere pleasure of poetic creation and melodic invention. He composes tales and idylls in verse, passages of pure description, satires, rhymed letters; he rehandles folk-ballads, and invents songs of his own in the same idiom:

> A faithless shepherd courted me,
> He stole away my liberty.
> When my poor heart was strange to men,
> He came and smiled and stole it then.
>
> When my apron would hang low,
> Me he sought through frost and snow.
> When it puckered up with shame,
> And I sought him, he never came.
>
> When summer brought no fears to fright,
> He came to guard me every night.
> When winter nights did darkly prove,
> None came to guard me or to love.
>
> I wish, I wish, but all in vain,
> I wish I was a maid again.
> A maid again I cannot be,
> O when will the green grass cover me?

He indulges in imitation of the literary models which his reading has discovered for him—of these imitations the most successful is his *Ode to Autumn*. It is written in imitation of Collins's *Ode to Evening*, but is nevertheless an original poem in its own right. In this way of writing, particularly, there lay danger for him; a false literary quality had completely swamped the slender talent of Bloomfield, and spoils page after page of Burns. But Clare miraculously escapes it. In describing nature, he always has his eye upon the object; his accuracy in detail is astonishing. Nor, when he depicts human life in the country, does he indulge in the conventional sentimentalities which he might easily have caught from eighteenth- and nineteenth-century bourgeois pastoralists.

It is true that he dwells here upon the more cheerful side of the picture; the strong moral realism of Crabbe is beyond his range, though he has left at least one poem in which the evil arising from enclosures is touched upon. Technically, also, Clare retains his unforced limpidity. His blank verse fragments are remarkably free and original; his couplets run with a natural gait that reminds us of Chaucer. He is often at his best when he is writing directly in the folk-tradition, as in most of his songs. The cast of his language—especially the syntax and word order, where a natural, unperiodic structure is the rule, and where inversions, when they occur, are never introduced with merely rhetorical intent—is one of the points in which he comes closest to Blake.

But it is in the poems that he wrote when confined in the asylum that Clare's genius shows itself most indisputably. In some of them he returns again to the observation and re-collection of external nature, but it is with a greater, often a strange intensity of vision. In such poems as *Clock-a-clay* (lady-bird) his own sensibility seems to be completely identi-fied with what he is describing. Some of the lyrics of this period, notably those connected with his more intimate emotions, attain, through his madness, to a visionary appre-hension of reality which is beyond the normal. Here again he is somewhat akin to Blake.

> I peeled bits of straw and I got switches too
> From the grey peeling willow as idlers do,
> And I switched at the flies as I sat all alone
> Till my flesh, blood, and marrow was turned to dry bone.
> My illness was love, though I knew not the smart,
> But the beauty of love was the blood of my heart.

Crowded places, I shunned them as noises too rude
And fled to the silence of sweet solitude,
Where the flower in green darkness buds, blossoms, and fades,
Unseen of all shepherds and flower-loving maids—
The hermit bees find them but once and away.
There I'll bury alive and in silence decay.

In such poems as these it is difficult to define rational meaning or even definite emotion; yet the intensity of passion is there. We seem to be listening to the voice not of a man but of a ghost—some spirit which has passed through and beyond suffering, so that it has somehow become impersonal, and part of the natural landscape against whose background it utters its lament.

It would almost appear as though Clare, who in his madness gave a detailed eye-witness account of the execution of Charles I, and of the Battle of the Nile, and declared that there was only one poet—Shakespeare, Milton, Byron, John Clare—possessed some genuine apprehension of states of being which transcend the personal, and had reached that borderline where hallucination passes into clairvoyance. Such a vision had always been implicit in his intense sensibility to the proper nature and life of natural objects; in some of his last poems it is expressed in notes of unequalled lyrical purity:

Love lives beyond
The tomb, the earth, which fades like dew!
I love the fond,
The faithful, and the true.

Love lives in sleep,
The happiness of healthy dreams:
Eve's dews may weep,
But love delightful seems.

'Tis seen in flowers,
And in the morning's pearly dew;
In earth's green hours
And in the heaven's eternal blue.

In Clare's the old, anonymous tradition of the English folk-poetry of the countryside suddenly becomes articulate in an individual voice. He is the last representative of that tradition, which in his own day powerful social and economic factors had disrupted. But also, as much as Blake or Shelley, Wordsworth or Coleridge, he claims a place in the authentic hierarchy of the English Romantic poets.

The story of Clare is without parallel in the subsequent history of English poetry. No other man, sprung directly from the peasantry, succeeded in overcoming the disadvantages of his birth, and at the same time displayed poetic gifts of a high order. But there are a few other poets of the nineteenth century who stand close enough in spirit to the folk-tradition to be considered its legitimate heirs. William Barnes was not a peasant but a schoolmaster, clergyman, and philological scholar. Yet his *Poems of Rural Life in the Dorset Dialect* are more than mere exercises in dialect writing; and though they are the careful work of a conscious artist (Barnes even drew upon his knowledge of Welsh and Persian poetry for some of his metrical devices) they often come very close, both in spirit and melody, to the genuine poetry of the peasantry.

Barnes was born about 1801, in the Vale of Blackmore. His father was a tenant-farmer, though his ancestors had once owned land of their own. He attended a village school, and later an endowed school at Stourminster. It seems that it was principally his delicate physique which prevented the poet from also becoming a farmer. He followed various professions—for example, copying deeds for a solicitor, and wood-engraving at a local printer's—and acquired his wide learning in spite of obstacles and through the assistance of friends. It was not till 1837 that he was able to put his name on the books of St. John's College, Cambridge, and not till 1862 that he was appointed to the living of Came. It is well-known that some of his philological views were somewhat eccentric—that he was a purist as regards the English tongue, and advocated the creation of such compounds as "Folkwain" (omnibus) "rimecraft" (arithmetic) to reduce the Latin element in the language. It is perhaps not so generally known that in his *View of Labour and Gold* he claimed to stand out for the teaching of the Mediæval Church concerning usury, in relation to the economic problems of his day. Like Clare, he deplores, in his "Eclogue" *The Common a-took in*, the system of enclosures whereby the landlords were ruining the life of the peasantry.

Barnes's poems display a very high level of general workmanship, and reproduce a wide range of scenes from the life of the countryman. They stand close enough to ordinary experiences, drawing their inspiration from simple and common emotions, occasionally from local traditions, customs, and superstitions. Passion (except in the beautiful poem on the death of his wife) and the sterner kind of realism are absent from them, though there is bitter irony in *The Common a-took in*, already mentioned, and its companion piece *Two Farms in Woone*. The melancholy which comes with recollection of the past, quiet affection in marriage, untroubled piety, a feeling for the beauty of nature, though not intellectualized—these, with rustic humour, are the prevailing notes, but softened, as though in the light of a fine summer's evening in the country. It is worth remarking that Barnes's poetry, as well as his philological experiments, are known to have influenced Hopkins. Hopkins's friend Coventry Patmore believed that Barnes and himself were the only two among the poets of the time in whom the great traditions of English poetry were continued. We do not readily think of them together, yet as in the author of *The Unknown Eros* and *The Angel in the House* the metaphysic of mysticism and the Romantic love of the Middle Ages are renewed, so in the Dorset parson we have almost the last voice of that village community whose traditions had their roots likewise in the mediæval constitution of society. The characteristics of the work of Barnes and Patmore are very different, yet each has that inner technical integrity, which enables the poet to

employ the simplest language and to describe the homeliest
domestic details without seeming flat or prosaic, which we
find in the great mediæval poets, and look for in vain in
Tennyson or Browning. It is this historical position of Barnes,
together with the lovely soft dialect which he employs,
which imparts to his poems a wistful sadness which is alien to
their subject-matter:

> Vor all the zun do leäve the sky
> And all the sounds of day do die,
> An' noo mwore veet do walk the dim
> Vield-path to clim' the stiel's bars,
> Yeet out below the rizen stars,
> The dark'nen day mid leäve behind
> Woone tongue that I shall always vind,
> A-whispering kind, when birds be still.
>
> Zo let the day come on to spread
> His kindly light above my head,
> Wi' zights to zee, and sounds to hear,
> That still do cheer my thoughtvul mind;
> Or let en goo, an' leäve behind
> An hour to stroll along the gleädes,
> Where night do drown the beeches' sheädes,
> An' grasses' bleädes, when birds be still.
>
> Vor when the night do lull the sound
> O' cows a-blearen out in ground,
> And sh'ill-vaic'd dog do stan an' bark
> 'Ithin the dark, bezide the road;
> An' when noo cracklen waggon's lwoad
> Is in the leäne, the wind do ring
> The merry peals that bells do ring
> O' ding-dong-ding, when birds be still.
>
> Zo teäke, vor me, the town a-drown'd
> 'Ithin a storm o' rumblen sound,
> An' gi'e me vaices that do speak
> So soft an' meek, to souls alwone;

The brook a-gurglen round a stwone,
An' birds o' day a zingen clear,
An' leaves, that I mid zit an hear
A rustlen near, when birds be still.

Contemporary with Barnes, and a similar figure in many respects, was Robert Stephen Hawker, the Vicar of Morwenstow in Cornwall. He, too, was something of an eccentric. He was not, however, of farming stock, nor is he so much the folk-poet, he is by the literary character of his work even more clearly a survivor from the Middle Ages cut off from the main stream of the nineteenth century.

A remarkable picture of Hawker, the man, and the parish in which he worked, is preserved in the well-known and very interesting biography of him by S. Baring-Gould. At the beginning of the nineteenth century, Morwenstow was a sufficiently remote place, where folk-tradition, superstitious or otherwise, was still firmly rooted, and the exploits of the wreckers and smugglers were a matter of living memory. It is clear that this virile and generous-hearted priest filled quite naturally and spontaneously his position as leader of the small, isolated community of farmers and fishermen, and was by them in like fashion accepted. His championship of the tenant-farmers against their landlords, and of the labourers against the farmers, is, like Barnes's views concerning usury, significant. The following appeal written by him in 1861, shows there was nothing vague or unpractical in Hawker's charity:

There are in Morwenstow about six thousand acres of arable land rented by seventy farmers; forty large and thirty small.

There are less than sixty able-bodied labourers and twenty-five half men at roads, etc.

With the proportion of one labourer to a hundred acres, there can be no lack of *employ*.

The rate of wages is eight shillings a week, paid not in money, but by truck of corn. A fixed agreement of a hundred and thirty-five pounds of corn, and eighteen gallons (commonly called seven scores) is allotted to each man in lieu of fourteen shillings, be the market price what it will.

A man with a wife and three or four children will consume the above quantity of corn in fourteen days. Therefore, such a man, receiving for his fortnight's work fourteen shillings worth of corn, will only leave in his master's hand one shilling a week, which one shilling usually is paid for house rent.

Now this inevitable outlay for the rent and loaf will leave—for fuel, for shoes, for clothing, for groceries, for tools, for club . . . Nil. £0. 0s. 0d.

But in the year 1860–61, the fourteen shillings paid for that corn will only yield in flour and meal ten shillings and sixpence, the millers being judges.

If a man have only a wife and two children to house and feed, his surplus money above his bread and rent will be one shilling (?) a week beyond the above example. But, in the recited list of exigencies, will that suffice?

It was from a knowledge of the state of the parish, that I assented to the collection, of which I enclose a statement.

Two farmers only had the audacity to allege that the effort was uncalled for, and a labourer of one of these must have gone barefooted to work the whole winter had not the money for a pair of shoes been advanced to him by the victim of the parish.

It appears to be a notion entertained by a chief patron of all our charities, that the wages and the treatment of the labourers at Kilkhampton are more favourable than in Morwenstow.
But, but, but—

What is the weekly wage?

How paid?

If in corn, at what price?

And are there contracts in other respects?

These are not questions which I want to be answered, but only questions for your own private consideration.[1]

Hawker and Barnes indeed fall short of systematic action in resistance to the economic injustices of the century, but their views of them, in so far as they impinged upon the village communities which they know, is clear enough.

[1] Quoted in *The Vicar of Morwenstow* by S. Baring-Gould.

Hawker had known Newman, Pusey, Ward, and Marriott at Oxford; but the peculiar romantic tone which his Anglicanism took lay apart from the main course of the Tractarian Movement and the Catholic Revival within the English Church. He dreamed of a restoration of the lost Celtic Church of Wales and Cornwall, and in his dress and the ritual of his services sought partly to adopt the usages of eastern Christianity, from which he believed (possibly erroneously) this Celtic Church to have taken its origin. Of the usages which he introduced into the ceremonies of his church, one—the Harvest Festival—has since become a custom generally adopted in the Church of England. It is characteristic of Hawker that this should be a festival in which the connection between the ritual life of the Church, and the seasonal rhythm of the crops and the countryside is emphasized. His mediævalism and romanticism were intense and genuine, the fruit of a visionary and poetic nature, no mere sentimental vagaries or picturesque quaintness, and one realizes how lonely must often have been his path.[1] He shared many of the superstitions of his parishioners and believed with a faith it would be wrong to deride in the direct and miraculous intervention of Divine Providence in his own affairs and those of his parish. He saw visions also, as Blake had done. Baring-Gould tells us that he wrote to Hawker questioning, on antiquarian grounds, whether St. Morwenna were really buried at Morwenstow. "What," replied the poet, "Morwenna not lie in the holy place at Morwenstow! Of that you will never persuade me—no, never. I know that she lies there. I have seen her, and she has told me as much, and at her feet ere long I hope to lay my old bones."[2]

Hawker as a poet is best known to most readers by his *Song of the Western Men—And shall Trelawney die?* It is a favourable, but by no means the most interesting, specimen

[1] On his deathbed he was received into the Roman Catholic Church, in circumstances which have given rise to some controversy.
[2] *The Vicar of Morwenstow.*

of the vigorous ballads he based upon local traditions. They are much more literary in style than the poems of Clare, even of Barnes, and frequently marred by a conventionality in diction. For though, by sympathy, so close to the peasantry, Hawker was not, even to the same extent as Barnes, one with them in speech and blood.

Hawker is a self-conscious antiquarian, with something of a nostalgia for the past. He is steeped in local legends and traditions. His ballads are most genuine, perhaps, when he captures in them something of that mixture of piety and superstition which enter into the religious emotion of the peasantry. Thus in *A Legend of the Hive* he tells the story of an old woman who stole the Host from the church, believing it would have a magical effect in checking a decline which had set in among her bees, and placed it in their hive. But to Hawker, with his instinctive symbolism, "the nation of the bees" are a "strange people . . . , a mystic race, in life, in food, in dwelling place".

> They first were seen on earth, 'tis said,
>   When the rose breathes in spring:
> Men thought her blushing bosom shed
>   These children of the wing:
> But lo! their hosts went down the wind,
> Filled with the thoughts of God's own mind.
>
> They built them houses made with hands,
>   And there alone they dwell:
> No man to this day understands
>   The mystery of their cell.
> Your mighty sages cannot see
> The deep foundations of the bee.

In this context, Hawker is able to raise the climax of his folk-legend, in which the bees build a kind of tabernacle of wax over the Sacrament, to a higher level of poetic significance. The extremely primitive idea of the mysterious and sacred nature of the bee, and the Christian conception of the

6

Sacrament, are brought into imaginative relation one with another.

But his most remarkable achievement is his blank verse epic fragment, *The Quest of the Sangraal*—which stands on a level above the best of his work. It seems to me that this is the most successful poem directly inspired by the Arthurian legend in English since the Middle Ages, and one of the most interesting poems of its period. We shall have to go to the poems of the great Romantics to find a like sense of the symbolism of the world of inward human experience combined with so strong a feeling for concrete realities. *The Quest of the Sangraal* appeared many years before Tennyson's *Holy Grail*, and Hawker thought that the more celebrated poet owed the idea of treating the Arthurian myth to a suggestion of his own, made when the future laureate paid a visit to the Cornish poet. Be that as it may, Tennyson's *Idylls* even at their best (and that is better than some suppose) in certain very important qualities fall short of Hawker's poem. Tennyson moves in perfect mastery of his exquisitely smooth, though languid-flowing blank verse; time after time he strikes out the lovely unforgettable phrase; but these things, however admirable, are the graces of poetry, which too many mistake for poetry itself. But Hawker pierces through to the true life and meaning of its subject-matter. The harmony of verse consists not primarily in the moulding of the form from without, but in an inner necessity of musical cadence.

Here is the beginning of the speech of Arthur in Tennyson's *Morte d'Arthur*, the earliest and best of his *Idylls*:

> Then spake King Arthur to Sir Bedivere:
> "The sequel of to-day unsolders all
> The goodliest fellowship of famous knights
> Whereof this world holds record. Such a sleep
> They sleep—the men I loved. I think that we
> Shall never more, at any future time,
> Delight our souls with talk of knightly deeds,

Walking about the gardens and the halls
Of Camelot, as in the days that were.
I perish by this people that I made—
Tho' Merlin sware that I should come again
To rule once more—but let what will be, be.
I am so deeply smitten thro' the helm
That without help I cannot last till morn.
Thou therefore take my brand Excalibur,
Which was my pride: for thou rememberest how
In those old days, one summer noon, an arm
Rose up from out the bosom of the lake,
Clothed in white samite, mystic, wonderful
Holding the sword—and how I row'd across,
And took it, and have worn it like a king:
And, wheresoever I am sung or told
In after time, this also shall be known:
But now delay not: take Excalibur,
And fling him far into the middle mere:
Watch what thou seest, and lightly bring me word."

It is expressed with consummate art, but we are not con-
vinced of the reality of the scene. We miss the accent of the
natural speaking voice; the archaisms are introduced with too
self-conscious an air, and the diction is forced. Such tumid
rhetoric as is illustrated by the tautologies: "We shall *never
more, at any future time . . . as in the days that were*" can only
arise when a poet is writing with no more than half his mind
on his subject-matter. Above all, the feeling in these lines is
tame—it does justice neither to the great hero of tradition,
Arthur, in the hour of his defeat, nor to the complex creature
that was Tennyson.

Note again the essentially commonplace content of the
well-known last speech of Tennyson's Arthur:

"The old order changeth, yielding place to new,
And God fulfils Himself in many ways,
Lest one good custom should corrupt the world.
Comfort thyself; what comfort is in me?

I have lived myself, and that which I have done
May He within Himself make pure! but thou
If thou should'st never see my face again,
Pray for my soul. More things are wrought by prayer
Than this world dreams of. Wherefore let thy voice
Rise like a fountain for me night and day.
For what are men better than sheep or goats
That nourish a blind life within the brain,
If, knowing God, they lift not hands of prayer
Both for themselves and those who call them friend?
For so the whole round earth is every way
Bound by gold chains about the feet of God."

Now listen to the voice of Hawker's Arthur, as he laments
the fate whereby he may not join his knights in their
high quest.

There the brown barrow curves its sullen breast,
Above the bones of some dead Gentile's soul:
All hushed—all calm—and cold—until anon
Gleams the old dawn—and well remembered day—
Then may you hear beneath that hollow cairn
The clash of arms: the muffled shout of war,
Blend with the rustle of the kindling dead;
They stand—and hush their hearts to hear the King.
Then said he, like a prince of Tamar-land,
Around his soul, Dundagel and the Sea:
"Ha! Sirs—ye seek a noble crest to-day,
To win and wear the starry Sangraal,
The link that binds to God a lonely land.
Would that my arm went with you, like my heart!
But the true shepherd must not shun the fold:
For in this flock are crouching grievous wolves,
And chief among them all, my own false kin.
Therefore I tarry by the cruel sea,
To hear at eve the treacherous mermaid's song,
And watch the wallowing monsters of the wave,
And all things fierce, and wild, and strange, alone.

"I have no son, no daughter of my loins,
To breathe, 'mid future men, their father's name,
My blood will perish when these veins are dry
Yet am I fain some deeds of mine should live,—
I would not be forgotten in this land:
I yearn that men I know not, men unborn,
Should find, amid these fields, King Arthur's fame!
Here let them say, by proud Dundagel's walls—
They brought the Sangraal back by his command,
They touched these rugged rocks with hues of God;
So shall my name have worship, and my land!

"Ah! native Cornwall, throned upon the hills;
Thy moorland pathways worn by angel feet,
Thy streams that march in music to the sea
'Mid ocean's merry noise, his billowy laugh!
Ah me! a gloom falls heavy on my soul—
The birds that sang to me in youth are dead;—
I think, in dreamy vigils of the night,
It may be God is angry with my land:
Too much athirst for fame: too fond of blood,
And all for earth, for shadows and the dream
To gleam an echo from the winds of song!

"But now, let hearts be high: The Archangel held
A tournay with the fiend on Abarium,
And good St. Michael won his dragon crest.

"Be this our cry: The battle is for God!
If bevies of foul fiends withstand your path,
Nay, if strong angels hold the watch and ward,
Plunge in their midst, and shout 'A Sangraal!' "

There speaks here not only the legendary hero, but the
lonely priest also, and the poet—so often fated to be to others
a means of grace in which himself may not participate. The
verse has not the limited perfection of Tennyson's, but a
rugged strength and a wild music of its own.

The vision of the Holy Grail is apprehended by Tennyson

with a scared and emotional mysticism which is very characteristic of him:

"Sweet brother, I have seen the Holy Grail
For, waked at dead of night I heard a sound
As if a silver horn from o'er the hills
Blown, and I thought, It is not Arthur's use
To hunt by moonlight, and the slender sound
As from a distance beyond the distance grew
Coming upon me—O never harp nor horn
Nor ought we blow with breath, nor touch with hand,
Was like that music as it came; and then

"Gleamed through my cell a cold and silver beam
And down the long beam stole the Holy Grail,
Rose-red with beatings in it, as if alive,
Till all the white walls of my cell were dyed
With rosy colours creeping on the wall;
And then the music faded, and the Grail
Past, and the beam decay'd and from the walls
The rosy quiverings died into the night."

In Hawker the meaning of the vision is at once more deeply felt, and more intellectually defined. It is a sign of the indwelling of God with men through the Incarnation, and at the same time an image of the productive and life-giving principle in creation. I do not think Hawker would have been disconcerted by those modern theories which find in the Grail the fertility symbol of a corn-cult. Only he would have seen further into the spiritual realities for which the manifestations of primitive religious feeling themselves furnish only an imperfect symbolism. Thus he speaks of Joseph of Arimathea, the Grail-keeper:

"He dwelt in orient Syria, God's own land,
The ladder foot of heaven—where shadowy shapes
In white apparel glided up and down!
His home was like a garner, full of corn
And wine and oil: a granary of God!

> Young men, that no one knew, went in and out
> With a far look in their eternal eyes!
> All things were strange and rare: the Sangraal
> As though it clung to some etheral chain,
> Brought down high heaven to earth at Arimathee."

Tennyson would like to have rejected and denied the divine vision. For him the coming of the Grail is a sign for the breaking of the Round Table, the prudential virtues which all that part of his nature most in sympathy with the uninspired Puritanism of the Victorian Age had built; and he makes his Arthur deplore the desire of his knights to follow the Quest. That sort of thing, one is given to understand, may be all right for Galahad, who is somehow a special case—but for the rest of the knights, the Quest was a mistake—all rather unhealthy. Here is Arthur's "I told you so" after the business is finished:

> "And spake I not truly, O my knights?
> Was I too dark a prophet when I said
> To those who went upon the Holy Quest,
> That most of them would follow wandering fires,
> Lost in the quagmire?—lost to me and gone,
> And left me gazing at a barren board,
> And a lean order—scarce returned a tithe—
> And out of those to whom the vision came
> My greatest hardly will believe he saw;
> Another hath beheld it afar off,
> And leaving human wrongs to right themselves,
> Cares but to pass into the silent life.
> And one hath had the vision face to face,
> And now his chair desires him here in vain,
> However they may crown him otherwhere."

Hawker is at once more courageous and more spiritually healthy. The challenge of the vision is accepted; his champions set out upon the Quest with joy and a sober courage (Hawker's knights are very real men; they have the healthy appetites of

the heroes of genuine primitive poetry) whatever forebodings
of danger and defeat may also lie behind.

And for all his mediævalism, Hawker's sense of his own age
is superior to Tennyson's. The latter apprehends the symbols
which he finds in Malory, emotionally only. When he attempts
to apply them by means of allegory to his own time he is dull
and uninspired, sometimes absurd. Hawker has a much
stronger sense at once of the proper life of the legendary
world which he describes, and the validity of the symbols
provided by it. His poem closes with a vision of the recovery
of the Sangraal by Galahad, and of the fate of Britain. This
is an allegory of the spiritual history of the country down to
the poet's own time, with its final protest against the materialism of the nineteenth century:

> "Ah haughty England! lady of the wave!"
> Thus said pale Merlin to the listening King;
> "What is thy glory in the world of Stars?
> To scorch and slay! to win demoniac fame,
> In arts and arms; and then to flash and die.
> Thou art the diamond of the demon crown,
> Smitten by Michael upon Abarim,
> That fell; and glared an island of the sea.
> Ah! native England! wake thine ancient cry,
> Ho! for the Sangraal! vanished vase of heaven!
> That held, like Christ's own heart, an hin of blood."
> He ceased: and all around the dreaming night
> There stood Dundagel, throned: and the great sea
> Lay, a strong vassal at his master's gate
> And, like a drunken giant, sobbed in sleep.

I hope I have quoted enough to illustrate the remarkable
qualities of this poem. But it must be read in its entirety before these can be fully felt.

This is perhaps the place to include a note on the
work of yet another country clergyman—Tennyson's elder
brother Charles, who took the name of Tennyson Turner on

succeeding to an uncle's estate, and was vicar of Grasby in Lincolnshire. It cannot be claimed that his work represents a continuation of the folk-tradition in the same sense as that of Barnes, or even Hawker, though the Tennysons had deep roots in the county of Lincolnshire, and were ultimately descended from yeoman stock. It is worth remembering that Alfred himself never quite lost a trace of his native Lincolnshire accent, and the poems in which he employs the dialect of that county—such as *The Northern Farmer*—are among the most vigorous and genuine of his productions. Charles's work consists almost entirely of a number of sonnets. He lacks his brother's suavity, and scarcely one of these sonnets is without some technical flaw; yet they live by their sincerity, and a certain sweetness and delicacy of mind which shines through them. The author is by turns innocent, learned, almost naively pious, scholarly, and a close and accurate observer of nature. His work is full of conceits—as when he compares the bright feathers on the head of the gold-crested wren to the final touch of beauty which adds perfection to the sonnet. Sometimes these strike out flashes of genuine imagination which go beyond anything his more famous brother could achieve. Thus, in *Nehemiah's Night Ride*, Nehemiah is represented as riding over the ruined site of Jerusalem, and hearing, as he does so, the dying sigh of Moses on Horeb, and the splash of a wave in the pool of Bethesda —all history, past and to come, is present in one moment of significant experience. But it is as a recorder of the traditional life of the countryside that he concerns us here. The editor of the selection of his sonnets published in 1931 in the *Augustan Books of Poetry* series justly describes them as "the most faithful picture verse has left of the old countryside of Church and hunt, squire and parson". Tennyson Turner is quite free from romantic or idyllic nostalgia. Hence he is also able to accept, quite naturally, the changes which mechanization brings into this country world, as in the two following sonnets on the steam threshing-machine:

I

Flush with the pond the lurid furnace burn'd
At eve, while smoke and vapour fill'd the yard;
The gloomy winter sky was dimly starr'd,
The fly-wheel with a mellow murmur turn'd;
While, ever rising on its mystic stair
In the dim light, from secret chambers borne,
The straw of harvest, sever'd from the corn,
Climb'd, and fell over, in the murky air.
I thought of mind and matter, will and law,
And then of him, who set his stately seal
Of Roman words on all the forms he saw
Of old-world husbandry: *I* could but feel
With what a rich precision *he* would draw
The endless ladder, and the booming wheel!

II

Did any seer of ancient time forebode
This mighty engine, which we daily see
Accepting our full harvests, like a god,
With clouds about his shoulders,—it might be
Some poet-husbandman, some lord of verse,
Old Hesiod, or the wizard Mantuan
Who catalogued in rich hexameters
The Rake, the Roller, and the mystic Van:
Or else some priest of Ceres, it might seem,
Who witness'd, as he trod the silent fane,
The notes and auguries of coming change,
Of other ministrants of shrine and grange,—
The sweating statue, and her sacred wain
Low-booming with the prophecy of steam!

These sonnets show, I think, that Tennyson Turner was more than just the recorder of the life he saw around him, but possessed a real sense of the organic continuity which is to be discerned, or should be, in all man's activities.

But there is a later poet, at once profoundly influenced by the regionalist and folk tradition, and occupying a central place in the current of nineteenth-century literature. The example and the personal friendship of Barnes encouraged another Dorset man, an architect by profession, but of the same stock of the well-to-do farmers by descent, to treat of the scene, life, and traditions of his native county. In Hardy's verse the cadences of folk-song and ballad and popular chapel hymn were to be echoed yet again. Despite the considerable extent of his reading, in ancient as well as in modern literature, it is clear that to a great extent Hardy's sensibility remained that of the unlearned countrymen he described. Even the plots of his novels, as Lord David Cecil has pointed out,[1] might in many cases be those of folk-ballads.

When we enter the world of Hardy's imagining, we have left behind us the dewy freshness of Clare, the genial evening sunshine of Barnes, the visionary twilight of Hawker. The misery of a countryside whose traditional culture has been damaged beyond repair is manifest in this bleak region where so often a cruel and ironic Fate walks abroad, and meets with so little resistance from the human spirit.

. The stature of Hardy as a poet (the novelist we need not here discuss, though his work in both kinds forms a natural unity) is difficult to estimate. The range of his work is far beyond that of the other poets dealt with in this chapter, but he is a less sensitive, or at least a less certain artist than his predecessors. I question much whether his actual poetic achievement in *The Dynasts* is equal to the impressiveness of the theme. It seems to me that Hardy lacked both an adequate technique and the requisite inherited cultural background for the successful performance of a work of epic proportions. The sense of history and of great heroic action is there, but Hardy's Universe, for all his "Overworld", is spiritually too circumscribed, and his verse has not the ritualistic pomp of diction which epic demands—that, alone of latter-day poets, Doughty was able to command without becoming either stilted or tumid.

[1] In his book *Hardy the Novelist*.

The Dynasts is greatly planned. But the verse is bare and wooden, like a schoolboy's imitation of Shakespeare; only the Wessex scenes really seem to come to life. It is worth noting how, even when he contemplates the great battles of history, Hardy's attitude remains essentially that of the countryman. His sense of pity before Waterloo, like that displayed by his successor, Edmund Blunden, in some of his war poems, is aroused as much by the thought of good and fertile land defiled, and the destruction of natural life in general, as by the individual suffering of human beings involved:

Chorus of the Years

Yea, the conies are scared by the thud of hoofs,
And their white scuts flash at their vanishing heels,
And swallows abandon the hamlet roofs,

The mole's tunnelled chambers are crushed by wheels,
The larks' eggs scattered, their owners fled;
And the hedge-hog's household the supper unseals,

The snail draws in at the terrible tread,
But in vain; he is crushed by the felloe-rim;
The worm asks what can be overhead,

And wriggles deep from a scene so grim,
And guesses him safe; for he does not know
What a foul red flood will be soaking him!

Beaten about by the heel and toe,
Are butterflies, sick of the day's long rheum,
To die of a worse than the weather-foe.

Trodden and bruised to a miry tomb
Are ears that have greened but will never be gold,
And flowers in the bud that will never bloom.

Chorus of the Pities

So the season's intent ere its fruits unfold,
Is frustrate, and mangled, and made succumb,
Like a youth of promise struck stark and cold! . . .

But what of these, who tonight have come?

It is in his shorter poems—his ballads and songs and re-
flective pieces—that Hardy is seen to the best advantage.
Besides what I have called the regionalist tradition, there is
one very clear influence upon these poems—that of Browning. Browning is in many ways the most urban and cosmo-
politan, and the most literary, widely and curiously read, of
all the Victorian poets. A poet himself, he is often the fav-
ourite of those persons whose sensibility is attuned primarily
to prose, and it is natural that the two poet-novelists of the
later part of the century, Hardy and Meredith should, in
verse, have divided his heritage.

It is the fusion of Browning's dramatic appreciation of the
value of situation and his intellectual curiosity, with the
countryman's sensibility, rooted in a traditional way of life,
nourished on the detailed observation of landscape and the
ways of animated nature, which gives to Hardy's poetry its
unique qualities. But his intellectual attitude is the product
of his age and of his environment. Hardy's ironic pessimism
is personal, but it can also be traced to his intuitive per-
ception of the social decay of the countryside in which he
grew up. From the philosophical point of view it has its
roots in that combination of a narrow scientific materialism
with an impoverished Puritanism which, for want of a
better faith, the late nineteenth century forced upon him.
The ruler of Hardy's universe is the cruel predestinating
deity of Calvinism, stripped of his anthropomorphic qualities
and theological trappings. He is also the amoral evolutionary
law of Huxley and Darwin. Hence, in spite of his genuine
poetic perceptions, it is questionable whether Hardy is a
great tragic artist. His people, peasants whose traditional
liberties (such as they were) have been taken from them, are
not sufficiently free. They are incapable of that sin of pride
of which according to the old poets, the tragic catastrophe
should be the consequence. They fall victims to the chances
which have been prepared for them by a malignant and un-
just, though impersonal, God. Yet spiritually impoverished

as Hardy's world is, his verse lives by its obvious sincerity. In him the old tradition puts forth its leaves once more, though the branches have become gnarled and wintry in the bleak social and intellectual climate which has fallen upon the countryside. It is notable that Hardy, not only in *The Dynasts*, but also in many of his stories and poems, harks back to traditions of the times of the Napoleonic Wars. Hardy's world, like that of Scott, in his Waverley novels, is a legendary one, in which traditions of a past generation are a thing more living than the actuality of the writer's own day.

If I am right in tracing a direct continuation of the traditional poetry of the peasantry in these nineteenth-century writers, that tradition practically comes to an end with Hardy. By the close of the century, the life of rural England had been too far disrupted, and the traditional songs of the countryside, with the traditional crafts and ways of life, were dead.

Yet there was a queer epilogue. In 1896, A. E. Housman, a classical scholar, and a reserved, possibly an emotionally twisted, and certainly an embittered man, found in a reminiscence of the dying countryside, and in the old songs of lads who were crossed in love, were hanged for crimes of jealousy or passion, or who marched away to fight in the French wars, an image of his own more personal sadness and frustration. Housman had little real or intimate connection, either by his birth or upbringing, with the countryside of which he sings. It is significant that he never went to Shropshire, but remembered seeing those distant hills lying to the west—like the sunset paradise of mythology—from the Worcestershire home of his childhood. The world of *A Shropshire Lad* is a literary pastoral dream-world of lost adolescence:

> Comrade, look not on the west:
> 'Twill have the heart out of your breast;
> 'Twill take your thoughts and sink them far,
> Leagues beyond the sunset bar,

—or again, still more poignantly:

> That is the land of lost content,
>   I see it shining plain,
> The happy highways where I went
>   And cannot come again.

Such verses tell their own story. The poems themselves were mostly written when Housman was living at Highgate and working in London, during the period of disappointment which followed on his failure to attain the distinction which undoubtedly should have been his in his final examination at Oxford. (Feeling that he had not done himself justice, he did not show up his papers, and thus took no degree.) If there is a more intimate personal emotion behind *A Shropshire Lad*, this must also be traced, I suspect, to an experience of his Oxford days.

The verse-forms employed by Housman appear, at first reading, as though they derived from folk-song and ballad; but the poet, with his ear attuned to Latin metres, has no real understanding of the free, lilting rhythms which are natural to English folk-poetry, as the monotonous regularity of his pauses, and his mechanical alternation of strong and weak accents, sufficiently prove. So also with the content of these poems: Housman assumes the simplicity of manner and emotional understatement of the ballad as a mask to conceal highly complex and sophisticated feelings of nostalgia and self-pity. He is not only an escapist, but lacks even the courage to affirm the dream-world which he has created. He introduces into his idylls, therefore, an ignobly cruel irony and a sniggering cynicism. Thus he seeks to belie even the sentimental values from which his poetry really takes its origin.

A Shropshire Lad was popular. Its pastoral atmosphere seemed like a fresh breeze after the jaded urbanism of the typical 'nineties poets. Housman's slick handling of words, together with his feeling for the evocative phrase which was all that readers, educated in the ever-narrowing taste of the central literary tradition of the Victorian era, had learned to look for as the hall-mark of poetry, gave to the poems the appearance of a perfection of style which, by more catholic standards, they do not really possess. The rank growth of pastoral lyricism which spread over English poetry during the next thirty years—the work of the so-called "Georgian" school—must be traced very largely to Housman's influence. It is a curious phenomenon, lying strictly outside the scope of this essay, but nevertheless the result of nineteenth-century rather than of twentieth-century literary tendencies. It is the poetry of the weekend cottage. The motor-car and the bicycle made access to the countryside, for the first time, widely possible for the urban middle-classes, and this superficial-picturesque holiday-writing had a wide appeal. Housman had inherited from the 'nineties poets a certain, though limited, care for style; most of his successors displayed neither this nor the slightest real knowledge of their subject-matter. Yet there were exceptions. W. H. Davies, son of the keeper of a public house, and in his early years living the life of a tramp both in England and America, wrote verses of a real freshness and simplicity, though he was rapidly spoiled by success. Edward Thomas was a genuine lover and observer of the countryside, though from without rather than as a countryman himself. In the detailed accuracy of his descriptive method he anticipated the manner of the urban journalistic poets of the 'thirties, and has probably been rather overrated in consequence. Victoria Sackville-West achieved something of a *tour de force* in her long poem *The Land*, reviving the eighteenth-century tradition of Georgic. Lastly, in the verse of Edmund Blunden we hear again the voice of a genuine countryman, though he has severed himself from his work and turned scholar; echoes of Clare's pure note and Hardy's quiet reflection:

> Though folks no more go Maying
> Upon the dancing green
> With ale and cakes and music loud
> To crown the fairest queen,

Yet little ones to each gate go
Before the clock tells noon,
And there the prettiest garlands show
That e'er Love smiled upon.

.   .   .   .

And for these little children
And my love like a child,
The May should never fade to-night
Could Time but be beguiled,
Could Time but see the beauty of
These singing honied hours,
And lie in the sun a dream while we
Hid up his scythe in flowers!

This tune is a very ancient one indeed. I do not think we
shall ever hear it thus again.

Chapter 3

THE POETRY OF DOUBT AND OF DESPAIR

THE poetry of Tennyson and Browning occupies a central position among the productions of their age. The work of each is wider in range than that of any other poet of their generation, and the popularity which it won, not over-rapidly, be it noted—in their own time, they have retained, on the whole, with the great mass of readers. Yet, despite its obvious merits, their poetry is intellectually unsatisfying. In the case of each of them, a troubled and fantastic imaginative vision underlies a creed whose formulated statements have little connection with it. They lived in an age when traditional ways of life and thought were being on all sides challenged. In the intellectual sphere, this challenge took the form of religious doubt, the nagging philosophical nightmare of the sensitive Victorian. It is obvious that Browning and Tennyson are—each in his own way—profoundly troubled by such doubt, the shadow of a more wide-reaching uncertainty, arising in an age of accelerated social change. Yet in their writings, though these contain so many long poems where arguments both for faith and against —particularly faith in God and in personal immortality—are put forward, they refuse on the last analysis quite to admit the extent to which they are affected by doubt. Hence the conclusion of *In Memoriam* fails to convince; and those poems of Browning such as *An Epistle from Karshish*, *A Death in the Desert*, *Caliban upon Setebos*, though they attempt a direct intellectual treatment of the question of the historical development of religion, have for all their brilliance something academic about them. They are writings round and about the subject, where neither intuitive faith nor honest doubt speaks clearly.

There seems to me to be little or no evidence in Browning's poetry that he was at all cognizant of the social evils and disruption of his day. Tennyson's more sensitive mind could not ignore them. But when he attempts to deal with them in *Maud* his reaction is scarcely adult, and his final refuge is in a hysterical jingoism.

Tennyson and Browning the "teachers" with a "message" for their Age, did not, on the whole, contradict that Age's own comfortable estimate of itself as one of progress and enlightenment; but the poet, which was one side of the nature of each, speaking out in moments of fear and nightmare, told another story.

Fundamentally, these two most eminent of the Victorian poets are dishonest. It is with a certain relief that we turn to the work of Matthew Arnold. He, at least, saw more truly the sickness of the Age and had the courage to record his vision:

> Ah, love, let us be true
> To one another! for this world, which seems
> To lie before us like a land of dreams,
> So various, so beautiful, so new,
> Hath really neither joy, nor love, nor light,
> Nor certitude, nor peace, nor help for pain;
> And we are here as on a darkling plain
> Swept with confused alarms of struggle and flight
> Where ignorant armies clash by night.

Arnold has abandoned the shelter of a traditional, consoling faith which his imagination could no longer accept, and has set out across the Darkling Plain. Read to-day, Matthew Arnold's prose works make some of us, at least, impatient with their author. Yet he sees the culture of the England of his day against a wider historical and European background than most of his contemporaries. He defines accurately its Philistinism. At a time when poetry was becoming more and more committed to an escapist attitude, he called for "criticism of life". Yet, when he attempts to be constructive, a kind of intellectual chill and numbness prevents the fruition of his thought. The shadow of his father, the great headmaster of Rugby, falls across the page, dictating the prim, pedagogic evangel which he puts forward. It is a hazy mixture of Germanized Hellenism and an Anglicanism excessively rarefied and with the bony structure of dogma removed.

So also in his poetry, there are two Matthew Arnolds—as there are likewise two Tennysons, two Brownings. But in Arnold the division is clearer, and the two voices do not, as in those poets, speak together continually, contradicting one another.

The nature of this duality can be illustrated by the relation of form to content in the work of the three poets. In Tennyson and Browning, the form is often forcibly superimposed upon the matter—conceived of as a mould to be applied from without, not as the inevitable incarnation of the thought. Hence the too regular blank verse of Tennyson's *Idylls*, the metronomic trochees of *Locksley Hall*, the jolting metres of Browning's later lyrics, his forced, pseudo-Elizabethan diction, his unnatural double and triple rhymes. In Arnold there is a real attempt to find new forms for fresh modes of thought, an attempt not often made in the Victorian Age. Yet his "free" metres get no further, as a rule, than a rather stiff blank verse, with lines of irregular lengths. In his finest work his sense of melody is beautiful; but at other times his emotional irritation gives to his work an uninspired stiffness and awkwardness, of which Browning at his most arid, Tennyson at his silliest, would have been incapable.

The two Arnolds can be seen together, almost consciously brought face to face and contrasted, in *Empedocles on Etna*. From the summit of the mountain the philosopher records his chilly, sad, confused estimate of life, in words where a grave poetry is not indeed absent:

We mortals are no kings
For each of whom to sway
A new-made world up-springs
Meant merely for his play.
No, we are strangers here; the world is from of old.

In vain our pent wills fret
And would the world subdue,
Limits we did not set
Conditions all we do.
Born into life we are, and life must be our mould.

Born into life: who lists
May what is false maintain,
And for himself make mists
Through which to see less plain:
The world is what it is, for all our dust and din.

Born into life: in vain,
Opinions, those or these,
Unaltered to retain
The obstinate mind decrees.
Experience, like a sea, soaks all-effacing in.

Born into life: 'tis we,
And not the world, are new.
Our cry for bliss, our plea
Others have urged it too.
Our wants have all been felt, our errors made before.

It is a note which sounds again and again through Arnold's verse—yet seldom with the same finality or intellectual intensity. It becomes more and more frequent as the years go by, and, falling lower and lower in pitch, degenerated into the flat prosaic aphorisms of the disheartened preacher—"a dandy Jeremiah", as someone described him. But from the lower slopes of the mountain, this voice is answered by that of the harp-player, Calicles. This is the other Arnold, and a

rarer, more adventurous poet. These songs have a pagan wildness, and at times even a note of cruelty arises from the very
lucidity of their inner vision. Most wonderful of all, I think,
is that which tells the story of Marsyas, the faun vanquished
by Apollo, and by him flayed—was he perhaps the Dionysian
singer silenced by the Apollonian intellect?—and of Olympus,
the poet, Marsyas's pupil, who loved him:

> At his master's piteous cries,
> Pressing fast with both his hands
> His white garment to his eyes,
> Not to see Apollo's scorn:—
> Ah, poor faun, poor faun! Ah, poor faun!

This is—here at its most poignant—the cry which sounds
again, more than once, in the most memorable passages of
Arnold's poetry; the lament of the lonely scholar for his lost
poetic *alter ego*—the forsaken Merman, crying unheard to
his bride from the troubled sea; the Scholar Gypsy, long
dreamed of but never found, in the lovely pastoral poem
which bears his name; Thyrsis, the mourned and missed
companion (Arthur Hugh Clough, indeed, but how much
more an image of Arnold's own soul) in its sequel—an elegy
which strives, with an art which has deceived many, to revive a forgotten spell. Such passages reveal Arnold, not as the
somewhat pedagogic classicist of Rugby and Oxford, but as a
highly romantic poet.

A certain mystery attaches to the group of lyrics entitled
Switzerland—the "Marguerite poems". Arnold himself is
said, in later life, to have declared to his daughter that
their subject was not autobiographical, but purely imaginary.
Arnold was, perhaps, more honest than the majority of
Victorian fathers, yet it is impossible to feel sure that he was
speaking the truth. But, for us, considering only his poetry,
the question as to whether the story they appear to enshrine
—of an affair with a girl in Switzerland who evidently had
other lovers as well—was fact or not, remains of secondary

importance. They serve, once again, to illustrate Arnold's profoundly romantic feeling of isolation and loss, of being separated from a part of his life:

> Yes! in the sea of life enisled,
> With echoing straits between us thrown,
> Dotting the shoreless, watery wild,
> We mortal millions live *alone*.
> The islands feel the enclasping flow,
> And then their endless bounds they know.
>
> Who ordered that their longing's fire
> Should be, as soon as kindled, cool'd?
> Who renders vain their deep desire?—
> A God, a God their severance ruled!
> And bade betwixt their shores to be
> The unplumb'd, salt, estranging sea.

It is perhaps worth noting, in passing, that, true or not, the "Marguerite" story offers a curious analogy with the real history of the relations between Wordsworth, one of Arnold's masters, and Annette Vallon—an episode which Wordsworth's Victorian biographers suppressed, and of which, therefore, Arnold himself must have been quite ignorant. Those who hold, with Mr. Herbert Read, that Wordsworth deserted Annette, and that this set up a permanent feeling of guilt in him, which played an important part in the subsequent development of his personality and his poetry (but I do not myself think we have enough evidence to warrant such an assumption) may, if they choose, postulate the development of a similar emotional complex in the case of Arnold.

It is interesting to compare the elegiac and epic idylls of Arnold with the *Hellenics* of Landor. The latter writer is, I think, the undoubtedly greater poet, and the more truly classical. He is, indeed, one of the very few English writers to whom the term can, without qualification, be applied.

Landor's work does not concern us here. Though he lived well on into the period which this book covers, he is a Regency poet of the generation of Wordsworth and Coleridge, and in spirit belongs to the eighteenth rather than the nineteenth century. He was an old-fashioned, aristocratic republican, and in his work exemplifies a kind of Classicism, rare in England but characteristic of the Continental movement of "enlightenment". Goethe, Alfieri, and Chénier provide the context in which he should really be considered. Nevertheless, a perusal of his poetry will serve to throw into stronger relief the essentially Romantic quality of Arnold. *Sohrab and Rustum* will, I guess, for a long time to come continue to find more readers than *The Last of Ulysses, Corythus, Chrysaor*, or even *Gebir*; and this for the strangely evocative beauty of such lines as the well-known concluding passage on the Oxus—lines which none, once having read, ever forgets:

> But the majestic river floated on,
> Out of the mist and hum of that low land,
> Into the frosty starlight, and there mov'd,
> Rejoicing, through the hush'd Chorasmian waste,
> Under the solitary moon: he flow'd
> Right for the Polar Star, past Orgunjé
> Brimming, and bright, and large; then sands begin
> To hem his watery march, and dam his streams,
> And split his current; that for many a league
> The shorn and parcell'd Oxus strains along
> Through beds of sand and matted rushy isles—
> Oxus, forgetting the bright speed he had
> In his high mountain cradle in Pamere,
> A foil'd circuitous wanderer:—till at last
> The long'd-for dash of waves is heard, and wide
> His luminous home of waters opens, bright
> And tranquil, from whose floor the new-bath'd stars
> Emerge, and shine upon the Aral sea.

It is clear that, despite their form, there is nothing "classi-cal", in any strict sense of the term, about these lines. The

Oxus is a symbol. To attempt to analyse it intellectually would be to destroy its beauty, for it suggests many meanings, all of which may contribute to its strong emotional effect: the course of the Soul, the Progress of Poesy (a river also, in Gray's *Ode*), the history of mankind itself. In his power of creating such a symbol—developing it so fully and minutely, yet at the same time always suggesting rather than defining —Arnold is unique in his generation; Browning would have argued round and about the concept; Tennyson might have glimpsed the image in a flash—he could not so have elaborated its significance. Arnold's method is rather to evoke—a method which might well be illustrated by his *Tristram and Iseult*. The latter is a most interesting experiment in form— part dramatic, part narrative, and where at times the action is commented on by an anonymous, and as it were, de-personalized chorus. Passion is here dealt with as subject-matter, yet the Victorian love of melodrama finds no place. The tragedy is seen obliquely, the emotions which exercise themselves around the bed of the dying Tristram suggested rather than stated. Finally, it is upon the figure of the other Iseult—Iseult of Brittany—who loves Tristram, yet who finds no place in his thoughts at the passionate crisis of his existence, that our interest is centred. The third part of the poem, which pictures her, many years afterwards, watching her children, and telling them the story of Merlin and Vivian, is treated with a beautiful, reserved tenderness, and ends on a note of romantic suggestion—apparently irrelevant to what has passed before, yet, artistically, how right:

> They sat them down together, and a sleep
> Fell upon Merlin, more like death, so deep.
> Her finger on her lips, then Vivian rose,
> And from her brown-lock'd head the wimple throws,
> And takes it in her hand, and waves it over
> The blossom'd thorn-tree and her sleeping lover.
> Nine times she waved the fluttering wimple round,
> And made a little plot of magic ground.

And in that daisied circle, as men say,
Is Merlin prisoner till the Judgment day,
But she herself whither she will can rove,
For she was passing weary of his love.

Arnold commands our respect, because he made no attempt
to close his eyes to the discouraging spectacle presented by
the loss of traditional faith and intellectual standards, but
went forward to find his own path across the Darkling Plain.
Yet some inhibition seems to have made it increasingly difficult for him to fix his intuitions in any adequate form. The
eyes of this poet are always turned backward in search of a
vision he has lost, and only momentarily recaptures. His note
of pensive melancholy, as he laments this failure, palls upon
us; and his verse, though it does not, at its best, lack music,
has a stiffness about it—indicative of the inner emotional
check that continually cramped the natural flow of his
inspiration.

Yet there is one poem, the product of his youth, in which
he seems to me to have attained, on this occasion only, to an
intensity of imaginative creation which transcends the limitations imposed upon him by his time and the inner conflict of his personality; a poem which combines, above all
other English verse of its age, a technical originality with a
freedom and naturalness of motion, which is an index of its
imaginative validity. Critics have dismissed *The Strayed
Reveller* as immature work. The appeal which it makes is a
personal one. Yet to me the rapid, natural, yet always musical
movement of the short, irregular, unrhymed verses, the
haunting loveliness of the scene—at once clear-cut and dream-
like—the vividness of the images which pass before the eyes
of the reader, have a quality of strange and fresh beauty like
nothing else in English poetry. The hushed portico of Circe's
palace, the goddess herself—female symbol of this poetic
inspiration—her "red creaming liquor, strown with dark
seeds", her companion, Ulysses, the "spare, dark-featured,

quick-eyed stranger", and the Reveller himself, the intoxi-
cated and enchanted boy; these, the marvellous succession of
pictures he calls up—of Tiresias "revolving inly The doom
of Thebes", the destruction of the centaurs, the Indian in his
drifting boat, the Scythian on the wide steppe, "for miles,
Alive with green lizards, And the springing bustard-fowl",
the merchants in the ferry-boat, the Heroes, "Sitting in the
dark ship on the foamless, long heaving violet sea"—

> Or where the echoing oars
> Of Argo, first
> Startled the unknown sea

—are brought before us, flashed upon the mind's eye in
concrete images, not by means of laborious detailed description. The theme of the poem, the product of these
images, not conveyed by any prosaic or didactic method, is a
real experience which no one, who has attempted, in however
humble a capacity, artistic creation, will deny. It is the intensity of the act of imaginative vision itself, the identity, in
that state of being, of subject and object—"to become what
we sing"—and the pain which this necessarily imposes upon
the finite human consciousness. This is the initial experience,
from which, it seems to me, all the remainder of Arnold's
poetry derives its strength, falling gradually to a more and
more subdued tone, as that impulse is lost. But here there is
no coldness, no numbness of feeling, no melancholy with its
suspicion of maudlin self-pity, as in even the best of the other
poems. Well might Arnold, in the person of the Reveller,
cry—

> But I, Ulysses,
> Sitting on the warm steps,
> Looking over the valley,
> All day long, have seen
> Without pain, without labour,
> Sometimes a wild-hair'd maenad,
> Sometimes a faun with torches;

> And sometimes, for a moment,
> Passing through the dark stems
> Flowing-robed—the beloved,
> The desired, the divine,
> Beloved Iacchus.

From the poetry of Matthew Arnold it is natural to turn to that of his friend Clough. He also discovered the Darkling Plain, and with more courage, and less looking backward, ventured to traverse it. But he was much more slenderly equipped, both as to imaginative and purely intellectual qualities. The conflict between the doubt engendered by his age and traditional faith was never resolved for him, and much of his work is dreary reading—mere self-torment and intellectual nagging. But he did not close his eyes to the social evils of the time; *The Latest Decalogue* hits hard, and hits in the right place. At his best Clough reintroduces into English poetry some of that sense of direct social reality which the satiric tradition, running through the eighteenth century down to Crabbe, and perhaps Byron, had possessed—but which Romanticism, concentrating upon inward states of experience, had tended to destroy. *Amours de Voyage* and *The Bothie* are very readable, lively, and pleasant poems; short verse-novels written in half-burlesque hexameters, and the hexameter is an impossible metre to take quite seriously in English, treating not only of human character and incident, but also of contemporary political and social issues, in a manner not pompous and rhetorical, not hysterical as in *Maud*, but with humour, intelligence, and also poetry. Clough is the Victorian forerunner of that school of poets who have attempted "social-realist" poetry in our own century. I believe that this colloquial, alert, unpretentious, yet vivid investigation of proximate reality is only a secondary function of poetry. But if the soil of the nineteenth century had contained more of this dry, gritty, salty element, there would have been fewer florid, hectic, rootless, parasitic growths sapping the intellectual strength of its literature.

Clough possesses, moreover, at his best, a faculty for straight-forward imaginative reasoning in verse, for genuine meta-physical poetry, such as had not appeared since the days of Pope (Wordsworth indeed is a great philosophical poet; but he is so by virtue of the personal lyrical experience he pre-sents. When he attempts dialectic—as in *The Excursion*—he fails). The following passage from *The Bothie*—in which Elspie, the Scotch peasant girl, answers her lover, Philip Hewson, the radical—shows Clough's combining towards the creation of poetry of no mean order:

> Well,—she answered,
> Quietly, after her fashion, still knitting,—Well, I think of it.
> Yes,—I don't know, Mr. Philip,—but only it feels to me strangely
> Like to the high new bridge they used to build at, below there,
> Over the burn and glen on the road. You won't understand me,
> But I keep saying in my mind,—this long time slowly with trouble
> I have been building myself up, up, and toilfully raising,
> Just like as if the bridge were to do it itself without masons,
> Painfully getting myself upraised, one stone on another,
> All one side I mean; and now I see on the other,
> Such another fabric uprising, better and stronger,
> Close to me, coming to join me: and then, I sometimes fancy,—
> Sometimes I find myself dreaming at nights about arches and
>   bridges,—
> Sometimes I dream of a great invisible hand coming down, and
> Dropping the great key-stone in the middle; there is my dreaming,
> There I feel the great key-stone coming in and through it,
> Feel the other part—all the other stones of the archway,
> Joined into mine with a clear happy sense of completeness,
>   tingling
> All the way up from the other side's basement-stones in the water,
> Through the very grains of mine—Just like, when the steel that
>   you showed us
> Moved to the magnet, it seemed a feeling got hold of them both
> —But this is confusion and nonsense. I am talking all things
>   I can think of,
> And you won't understand me, Mr. Philip.

The Bothie, which Clough called a "Pastoral", reflects his
Oxford period, before the doubts which were finally to drive
him into spiritual exile, became too insistent. It was inspired
by the hexameters of Longfellow's *Evangeline*, which Clough
had been reading aloud to his sisters, and is a light-hearted
poem, with something of the air of a mock-heroic. It tells the
story of a reading-party of undergraduates, such as Clough
himself had several times conducted, in the Highlands of
Scotland, and lightly touches upon the problems of Socialism
which were beginning to get the air at the time. *Amours de
Voyage*, its successor is, perhaps, a more serious work, though
the same welcome lightness of touch is preserved. All pre-
tence of using the hexameter as an equivalent of the classical
heroic line is now thrown away, but it becomes an admirable
poetic vehicle for English colloquial speech rhythms. It is
hard for the modern reader to believe that this poem was
written a century ago. The central figure of the poem,
Claude, is a young, sceptical intellectual, who witnesses, as
Clough himself had done, the siege of the Roman republic in
1849. His emotions in the face of war, bloodshed, and immanent danger are treated realistically, ironically, even cynically
—a piquant contrast to the unreal and rhetorical heroics to
which the age was too often prone:

> Now supposing the French or the Neapolitan soldier
> Should by some evil chance come exploring the Maison Serny
> (Where the family English are all to assemble for safety),
> Am I prepared to lay down my life for the British female?
> Really, who knows? One has bowed and talked, till, little by little,
> All the natural heat has escaped of the chivalrous spirit.
> Oh, one conformed, of course; but one doesn't die for good manners,
> Stab or shoot, or be shot, by way of graceful attention.

Here the tone of the verse is deliberately lowered to the
level of the conversational. But Clough, in the same poem,
can raise his hexameter into the expression of a lyrical
nostalgia when his subject demands it:

Tibur is beautiful, too, and the orchard slopes, and the Anio
Falling, falling yet, to the ancient lyrical cadence;
Tibur and Anio's tide; and cool from Lucretilis ever,
With the Digentian stream, and with the Bandusian fountain,
Folded in Sabine recesses, the valley and villa of Horace:—

In Arnold and Clough we encounter a characteristic
Victorian mentality—that of the Wistful Unbeliever, unable
to square his intellectual convictions with the traditional
faith he has lost, whose passing he continually mourns. From
such an attitude—fundamentally inconsistent and sentimental—great poetry cannot be expected to spring. Something more strenuously intellectual, a recapturing of lost
metaphysic, or a more desperate and courageous denial, were
necessary. In one poem of the period, this absolute rejection,
not only of faith, but also of hope, is made; and *The City of
Dreadful Night*, approaches, in my opinion, near to being
great poetry.

James Thomson, the author of this poem, belonged to a
world very different from that in which Arnold, Browning,
and Tennyson dwelt, or the not uncomfortable Bohemia of
the pre-Raphaelites. He was born in Port Glasgow in 1834,
on the 23rd of November. His father was a merchant seaman,
who in 1840 was permanently disabled by a stroke, which
not only made him incapable of supporting his wife and
children, but also enfeebled his mind, and made him subject
to fits of melancholy depression. His wife, the poet's mother,
was probably of a temperament to exercise a lasting influence
on her son's psychological make-up, though she died when he
was aged only eight. She is described as highly emotional and
imaginative, with a gloomy and narrowly religious disposition.
She was a member of the sect called "Irvingites". Examined
from the point of view of modern psychology, the poetry
of Thomson certainly appears to suggest that he was the
victim of some strong emotional influence in early childhood; nevertheless he was, at an early age, removed to the

impersonal atmosphere of the Royal Caledonian Asylum, an orphanage for seamen's children, where he was brought up. In 1850 he entered the Royal Military College, Chelsea, to be trained for the profession of an Army schoolmaster. During this period he became acquainted, not only with the work of Byron and Shelley, but also with French, German, and Italian literature. This is important; if we compare the later poetry of Thomson with that of Tennyson or with other poets who were more fortunate than he in their education, we are forced to admit that the former is marred by faults of style we can only characterize as provincial. Nevertheless, he shows to an extraordinary degree that he was able to profit by his contacts with foreign literature. The work of Novalis, Leopardi, and Heine finds a real echo in his poetry, and this places him closer to the main stream of European Romanticism than any other of the Victorian poets; it is these last who are, in a profounder sense, provincial.

In 1851 Thomson was sent to take up a post in a garrison school at Ballincollig, County Cork, in Ireland. Here he first met Matilda Wellar, the daughter of an armourer sergeant of a regiment stationed there, with whom, at the age of eighteen, he fell violently in love—though she herself was only thirteen at the time. Her death, only two years later, was a great shock to the poet. She became for him, as did his "bride" for Novalis, the representative of that archetypal figure of early departed youth and innocence, which haunts the poetry of the Romantics. It is her image, under different forms, which recurs in *The City of Dreadful Night*, and in many other of Thomson's poems.

At Ballincollig also began his friendship with Charles Bradlaugh, who was then serving as a soldier, but was later to become the fighting atheist and reformer. This was to lead to a no less important, if less profound, influence on the course of his life. Thomson, however, after a year returned from Ireland to the Training College at Chelsea, where he completed his course, and finally enlisted as an Army schoolmaster in 1854.

In this capacity he seems to have begun what promised to be a moderately successful career. He served in various parts of the British Islands, and at the same time found leisure both for extensive reading and for original composition. His work began to appear in periodicals under the pseudonym "B.V." (Bysshe Vanolis—in allusion to his two favourites among the poets, Shelley and Novalis), especially in Bradlaugh's *The National Reformer*. In 1862, however, he was discharged from the Army for some small infringement of discipline. From now onwards till his death in 1882 he had no fixed employment. Bradlaugh befriended him, and he wrote increasingly for *The National Reformer*, but finally a infringement opened between them. Other journalistic work took him to Spain as a war correspondent, and he was also for a short time in America as secretary to a mining company. It is noteworthy that he was one of the first champions of Whitman's poetry in England. His fortunes, however, continued to decline. The end of his life appears to have been wretched, attended by destitution, chronic drunkenness, and melancholia. *The City of Dreadful Night* appeared first in Bradlaugh's paper in 1874, different parts being printed in successive numbers, but did not find a publisher till 1880. This poem at last brought Thomson to the notice of the critics of the day, but he was now broken in health and spirits, and had only two more years to live. He died in London University Hospital, where he had been taken from the lodgings of Philip Bourke Marston, the blind poet.

His poems, other than *The City of Dreadful Night*, do not call for much serious consideration. Some may be regarded as imperfect essays in the mood of his masterpiece. His lighter verses, such as *Sunday up the River* and *Sunday at Hampstead* sometimes sink to incredible depths of vulgarity:

> My shirt is of the soft red wool,
> My cap is azure braided,
> My two white hands so beautiful,
> My tie mauve purple-shaded.

Both in form and style *The City of Dreadful Night* is strikingly different from all other Victorian poems. It consists of a series of cantos written in an eight-line stanza, descriptive of the City itself, which alternate with episodes composed in a variety of different metres. This structure gives to the whole poem a unity akin to that of symphonic music, while at the same time opportunities are given for the introduction of passages whose forms are subjectively determined.

The style and diction have been stigmatized as flat—and so they will seem to those who look only for the thrilling evocative phrases, whose taste has been formed by a preference for the self-conscious richness of imagery provided by Tennyson. In fact, the style of Thomson's poem, though unequal and not always free from the crudities of his early work, is in general excellent. The verse has a slow, sonorous movement, produced largely by the skilful placing of Latin polysyllables. The language is largely free from affectation and inversions. The poet's visual sensibility is acute, and the imagery he employs is always precise and concrete; there is little vague rhetoric. The apparent plainness arises from the pictorial method characteristic of Thomson. He builds up, often through a number of stanzas, a single visual image, often of a striking magnitude, and it is these images which are the units of his poetry. In this he is akin to the mediæval poets who followed the method of allegory—a tradition carried on by Spenser. Since Spenser, English poetry has tendered to rely for its effects, not upon the carefully built-up word picture, but on the skilful employment of phrases. Readers schooled in this latter manner often fail to appreciate the true poetic greatness of Chaucer and Spenser, and it is not to be wondered that Thomson's style has likewise been misunderstood.

Thomson was able to make use of the plainest words without falling into flatness, partly, no doubt, through his study of the crystalline Italian of Dante and Leopardi, but also, I think, because of the extreme consistency of his intellectual position. His utter rejection of religious belief becomes itself a sort of inverted dogma, and he is able to use words as precisely, and with as accurate and significant effect as the mediæval poets who wrote with the force of a universally accepted metaphysic underlying their use of language.

This leads us to one of the most remarkable features of the poem. Although it deliberately rejects all religious faith, and there is none of the sentimental repining of Arnold, Clough, or Hardy, this poetry is itself the product of a religious mind. In describing the city of dreadful night into which nineteenth-century scientific scepticism had driven him, Thomson unconsciously defines a state, where, in theological terms, God is immanent, but where his power is not actively revealed—precisely the character given in orthodox doctrine to Hell itself. The continual protest of his spirit against the City implies the existence of its opposite; and everywhere a kind of inverted religious symbolism is detectable.

In the passage following immediately upon the section in which Thomson gives his first general description of the City, one marked feature of his style is immediately apparent. Though the poem is represented as a dream, the images have an extraordinary concreteness and reality of detail. The City, with its "great piers and causeways, many noble bridges", its street-lamps which always burn, is a modern, nineteenth-century industrial city—the Glasgow of Alexander Smith's terrible poem, or the London of Thomson's later sufferings —seen through the darkened curtain of nightmare; not merely a romantic, hazy place where:

> Shrines and palaces and towers—
> Time-eaten towers that tremble not—
> Resemble nothing that is ours

—as in Poe's *City of the Sea*. It is this bringing together of the dream-symbol and the object of waking experience which gives to Thomson's poem a power not found in the dream-poetry of Shelley and Keats, and links him to the mediæval writers of allegory. Dante displays the same detailed preciseness, and makes continually a like direct reference to the scenery and landscape of the normal world with which his readers were familiar, in describing Hell.

In this same Canto an atmosphere not only of gloom and hopelessness but also of sterility is suggested by the "salt tides" of the river that surrounds the city, the "waste marshes" that "shine and glitter to the moon" beyond, the trackless wilderness that lies to the north and west. Pictures such as these make up the main theme of the poem, culminating in the great transcription of Dürer's *Melancholia* with which it closes—the vast, brooding mother-figure which is, significantly, the presiding goddess of the place. From these recurring visions the sharp, episodical passages detach themselves, and, miraculously, redeem the poem from monotony. Though there is not quite "all the sad variety of Hell" (in Dryden's phrase), yet there is some approach to it. There is not, as in the true *Inferno*, an intellectual progress in Evil: in this circle only one of the seven deadly sins presides, and is its own punishment, *Accidia*. The inhabitants, of whom the first to be introduced to the reader—the man who continually revisits the ruined shrines of "dead Faith, dead Hope, dead Love," is the type—for ever tread the same eternal round of misery.

The preciseness of the intellectual statement conveyed by the last-mentioned episode, the first of the particular incidents with which the poem is diversified is noteworthy:

> As whom his one intense thought overpowers,
> He answered coldly, "Take a watch, erase
> The signs and figures of the circling hours,
> Detach the hands, remove the dial-face,
> The works proceed until run down; although
> Bereft of purpose, void of use, still go."

There is a similar quality in a later episode: the vision of a

sculptured angel, winged and holding a sword, which is confronted by a stone sphinx. From the angel fall first its wings,
next its sword, leaving it an unarmed man with impotent
raised hands. Then the human figure itself crashes to the
ground, and lies broken beneath the feet of the implacable
and immobile sphinx.

Very different, both from scenes such as the foregoing, and
each other are the two passages in which the early death of
Matilda Weller is alluded to. The first is the story told by
the traveller who has come through the desert. Here the
images of violence and cruelty—the "bleeding eyeless
socket" presented by the eclipsed sun, the "hoarse and heavy
and carnivorous breath" of distorted animal forms that pursue
the speaker and pluck at him from the bushes with "sharp
claws, swift talons, fleshless fingers cold"—combine to produce a nightmare atmosphere. Into this enters a figure
which seems to promise love—a woman who carries, instead
of a lamp, her own bleeding heart. But she vanishes,
and bears away the better part of the pilgrim with her,
leaving what remains of him only to renewed and augmented
despair.

In the second of these two episodes the poet enters a
mansion whose windows, in striking contrast to all the others
in the City, are ablaze with light. He finds it hung everywhere with images of the same beautiful woman, and finally
comes upon a young man who, clasping a crucifix, mourns
before the dead body of his beloved, the Lady of the images.
The lyric put into his mouth has a simplicity which is exceedingly moving:

> The chambers of the mansion of my heart,
> In every one whereof thine image dwells,
> Are black with grief eternal for thy sake.
>
> I kneel beside thee and I clasp the cross,
> With eyes for ever fixed upon that face,
> So beautiful and dreadful in its calm.

I kneel here patient as thou liest there;
As patient as a statue carved in stone,
Of adoration and eternal grief.

While thou dost not awake I cannot move;
And something tells me that thou wilt not wake,
And I alive feel turning into stone.

Most beautiful were death to end my grief,
Most hateful to destroy the sight of thee,
Dear vision better than all death or life.

But I renounce all choice of life or death;
For either shall be ever at my side,
And thus in bliss or woe be ever one.

Not only the subject of this scene, but the atmosphere of luxury—the fragrant garden lawn and high trees that surround the mansion, the heavily draped hall, balustrade and broad stairway within—recall many similar passages in Poe's prose. Both men, be it noted, lost their mothers at about the same early age, and the obsession with the death of a beautiful, beloved woman which haunts their work, can, psychologically, doubtless be related to this event, and points to the existence of a similar type of abnormal mentality in both.

Like Poe, Thomson shows us the obverse side of Puritanism (Novalis also had a Puritan upbringing). They take us behind the façade of the century's material prosperity and liberal smugness to a Waste Land whose existence was not yet suspected. The sexual repression and distortions to which the manners of the age conduced had doubtless much to do with this underworld of nightmare. The following lines in *The City of Dreadful Night*—

The phantoms have no reticence at all:
The nudity of flesh will blush though tameless,
The extreme nudity of bone grins shameless,
The unsexed skeleton mocks shroud and pall.

are highly significant. They illuminate not only Thomson's own work, but much else in the literature of an age which loved to dwell upon funerals and death-bed scenes, in which melodrama pervaded novel and poem, and the writing of ghost stories and tales of horror was brought to a fine art.

In the intellectual quality of his poetry Thomson is the superior of Poe—though lacking the peculiar analytical mind revealed in the latter's prose. The ally of Bradlaugh, whatever his failings, avoided the vague aestheticism of the rootless American. In some respects Thomson comes nearer to a greater poet—to Poe's disciple, Baudelaire, another explorer of the underworld. The claim that he was, unconsciously, and by temperament, at bottom a Christian and Catholic spirit, delineating an evil whose very existence implied the possibility of its opposite, has been made for Baudelaire and could be made for Thomson. It is curious to observe on how many occasions the latter makes use of religious imagery—as when, in the vast cathedral which stands in the centre of the City, the inhabitants gather to listen to the words of a prophet; one who has penetrated the ultimate secrets of existence. He has brought back from the beyond a message—not indeed of hope, but only of the certainty of despair; this figure suggests, nevertheless, a kind of inverted Messiah.

Thomson's imaginative vision, like that of his master, Shelley, transcends the crude rationalism which is his intellectual starting-point. Like his own traveller, he strides austere, having neither hope nor fear. Although he does not know it, with his courage he has all but traversed the Darkling Plain. He is within reach of gaining a new intelligible vision of the universe, for which the images of the faith he had abandoned will once more provide a relevant symbolism.

Chapter 4

THREE ROMAN CATHOLIC POETS

THE confusion and uncertainty of style, the frequent
sense of nervous strain conveyed by the imagery and,
in particular, the imperfect relation between content
and form, which we have found characteristic of so many of
the Victorian poets, must be imputed in part to their failure
to discover a metaphysic adequate to their imaginative
intuitions. The science of the age tended more and more to
admit as valid only those truths which were verifiable by
its own experimental method, while philosophy tended to
abstract itself from existence, so that, though its predomi-
nant tone was idealistic, it offered no basis for an imaginative
world-view. Those among the poets who attempted to compromise with the scientific spirit of the age falsified their art
in proportion as they submitted to that spirit. For it refused to
take into consideration the possible validity as truths, no less
important than those arrived at by experiment, the intuitions
to which the poet's art owed its very existence. In the later
decades of the century, however, many of the poets withdrew from the contemplation of external reality into a region
of merely decorative beauty. Their intellectual position was
often one of active hostility to science, and they thus found
themselves isolated more and more from the educated public
upon whom the practical triumphs of the experimental
method were progressively obtruding themselves.

The idea that there was a necessary enmity between poetry
and science—held, for instance, by Rossetti, and by some of
the minor poets of the closing decades of the century—was a
peculiar, and a late development of Romantic sentiment.
Such earlier Romantic poets as Coleridge and Shelley had
been intensely interested in the science of their day, and it

contributed, along with Idealistic and Platonic philosophy a characteristic tinge to the thought and imagery of at least the latter of these two. In Shelley's poetry the concepts of science are treated imaginatively and with passion, in a way which is altogether different—though it is not easy to define this difference—from Tennyson's attempt to base a creed of hope for humanity on the contemporary scientific doctrine of progress. But the beginning of another attitude can be discerned in Keats, the Romantic poet most admired by the pre-Raphaelites, and who was regarded by them (rightly or wrongly) as in some sort the forerunner of the Aesthetic Movement of the later part of the century. It was Keats who complained that philosophy would clip an angel's wings, and unravel the woof and texture of the rainbow. The same complaint is taken up by Poe, who stands much more certainly in the line along which aestheticism was evolved:

Science! true daughter of Old Time thou art!
   Who alterest all things with thy peering eyes.
Why preyest thou thus upon the poet's heart,
   Vulture, whose wings are dull realities?
How should he love thee? or how deem thee wise,
   Who wouldst not leave him in his wandering
To seek for treasure in the jewelled skies,
   Albeit he soared with an undaunted wing?
Hast thou not dragged Diana from her car?
   And driven the Hamadryad from the wood
To seek a shelter in some happier star?
   Hast thou not torn the Naiad from her flood,
The Elfin from the green grass, and from me
The summer dream beneath the tamarind tree?

The Roman Catholic Church, however, still offered, to those who were prepared to accept her dogmas, a metaphysical system inherited from the earlier and more universal culture of the Middle Ages. She offered along with this, a body of myth and symbol, of ritual and sacrament—concrete images which yet made the strongest subjective appeal to the emotions. Lastly, Catholicism provided a sense of belonging to a corporate body, a community, though a restricted one, all of whose members shared the same basis of belief and action.

To the Romantic poet in particular, seeking to reconcile the findings of his imagination with his general conception of Reality, Catholicism furnished a powerful attraction. This will be very clearly seen if we examine the history of the Romantic movement in poetry as it manifested itself on the Continent. Though Romanticism began as a child of eighteenth-century enlightenment, and of Rousseau's affirmation of the passions, a reaction in favour of the outward forms of Christianity and Catholicism soon began to play a part in it —the most explicit manifestation of which is, of course, the aesthetic Catholicism of Chateaubriand's *Le Génie du Chrétianisme*. In Germany, Heine, in his famous essay on *The Romantic School*, specifically intensifies the principles animating that school with those of mediæval Christian art, as opposed to that which was Classical and Pagan. "It was a passion-flower which had blossomed from the blood of Christ." In Germany, Romanticism was, indeed, equated by many critics, not with the ideals of the French Revolution, but with Catholic reaction. In France, on the other hand, it tended, politically, or ecclesiastically, to lead to a new Catholic Liberalism, such as that of Lammenais. In the history of English Romanticism we can detect parallel tendencies to these, though their nature is superficially obscured by the different position of the Roman Catholic Church in England, and by the Catholic claims of the Church of England itself, which had never been quite forgotten, and which were to be revived by the Oxford Movement of the thirties and forties of the nineteenth century.

At the very beginning of the Romantic Movement we find the Gothic monuments of St. Mary Redcliffe exercising their spell on the youthful Chatterton, who shortly before his death is said to have declared his belief that the Church of

Rome was the true Christian Church. The monuments of Westminster Abbey exercised a similar influence on Blake, when, as a young engraver's apprentice, he was set to make drawings of them. Blake's religious intuitions, however, led him to a formulation of belief which, on the surface, appears to have little in common with the orthodox confession of any church. The same may be said of the other poets of the Romantic Movement proper—both in England and abroad —notably Hölderlin and Gerard de Nerval. These touch religious experience at a far deeper level of reality than do such writers as Lamartine or Chateaubriand. But the time had not yet come—if indeed it is ever to come, when such imaginative discoveries were to be reconcilable with orthodoxy. But about the orthodoxy of the less adventurous there hangs the unreality which springs from nostalgia and picturesqueness.

The connection between the Oxford or Tractarian Movement and poetic Romanticism is not obvious on the surface. The leaders of the Oxford Movement were primarily interested in theology, and the theology they sought to revive was patristic, not mediæval. Nevertheless, the connection existed. The Romantic mediævalism of Scott, of whom all his life Newman was a reader and admirer, had done much to instil into the minds of Englishmen an idealization of the past, and an attachment—very foreign to the mentality of the preceding generations—to the picturesqueness of traditional ritual. This was clearly recognized by the fanatical anti-Tractarian, George Borrow, who wrote: "Whence did the pedants get the Popish nonsense with which they have corrupted youth? Why, from the same quarter from which they got the Jacobite nonsense with which they have inoculated those lads who were not inoculated with it before—Scott's novels. Jacobitism and Laudism, a kind of half-Popery, had at one time been very prevalent at Oxford, but both had been long consigned to oblivion there, and people at Oxford cared as little about Laud as they did about the Pretender. Both were dead and

buried there as everywhere else, till Scott called them out of
their graves, when the pedants of Oxford hailed both—ay, and
the Pope, too, as soon as Scott had made the old fellow
fascinating enough through particular novels, more especially
The Monastery and *The Abbot*." The influence of Scott can
be seen clearly enough in such Anglo-Catholic literary docu-
ments as the novels of Charlotte Yonge, and in Shorthouse's
philosopho-religious romance, *John Inglesant*.

But on a deeper level, germs of this particular revival of
religious feeling are to be sought in the influence of Wordsworth and Coleridge—though the name of the latter, as a
religious philosopher, is generally connected with the genesis
of the Broad Church rather than the High Church Movement. One of the strongest impulses towards the Oxford
Movement was contributed by the verse of Keble's *Christian
Year*. Newman in his *Apologia* tells us how this brought home
to him "what may be called, in a large sense of the word, the
Sacramental system; that is, the doctrine that material
phenomena are both the types and the instruments of real
things unseen, a doctrine which embraces not only what
Anglicans as well as Catholics believe about Sacraments
properly so called, but also the article of 'the Communion
of Saints' in its fullness: and likewise the Mysteries of the
Faith". He goes on to speak of the connection of this philosophy of religion with what is sometimes called "Berkeleyism"
—and we may take him to understand by this, not only the
system of Berkeley, but Idealist philosophy in general,
including that of Kant, whose name he associates with that
of Berkeley in another passage. Of all such Idealist thought
Coleridge had been the great disseminator in England, Keble
himself was undoubtedly influenced by Wordsworth, whose
friendship he enjoyed. The Sacramental attitude to the
natural universe is the prime intuition which informs and
is implicit throughout the poetry of Wordsworth and
Coleridge, even where it admits of a Pantheist, rather than
a Christian interpretation. Miss Edith Batho, in her most

valuable book, *The Later Wordsworth*, has shown that Wordsworth's philosophy of Nature, though it received an impulse
from the Idealism of Coleridge, was deeply rooted in the old-
fashioned eighteenth-century High Anglicanism in which, in
his youth, he had been trained. His later orthodoxy may be
considered, not so much as an apostasy from his Romantic
pantheism, as a return to these roots. He was conscious of,
and in sympathy with, the aims of the Tractarians. Among his
later work, *The Ecclesiastical Sonnets*, though on the whole
feeble as poetry, are noteworthy as showing his attitude
to the mediæval Church. (It is, incidentally, remarkable
that he was ahead of the historians of his time in divining the
true greatness of St. Francis of Assisi.) Wordsworth himself
said that in *The Ecclesiastical Sonnets*, written in the 'twenties,
he had anticipated the Oxford Movement by a decade. His
sonnet on the Virgin is worth quoting by way of illustration;
he is speaking of the Reformation:

> Mother! whose virgin bosom was incrost
> With the least shade of thought to sin allied;
> Woman! above all women glorified,
> Our tainted nature's solitary boast;
> Purer than foam on central ocean tost;
> Brighter than eastern skies at daybreak strewn
> With fancied roses, than the unblemished moon
> Before her wane begins on heaven's blue coast;
> Thy Image falls to earth. Yet some, I ween,
> Not unforgiven the suppliant knee might bend,
> As to a visible Power, in which did blend
> All that was mixed and reconciled in Thee
> Of mother's love and maiden purity,
> Of high with low, celestial with terrene!

The career of the Irish poet, Aubrey de Vere, who began as
a younger disciple and friend of Wordsworth, under whose
influence his verse (much of which is of considerable merit,
and deserves to be better known) was written, and who passed
through Anglo-Catholicism to a final adherence to Rome, is

significant. It was de Vere's influence which was largely responsible for his friend Patmore's conversion to Roman Catholicism.

But this book is concerned solely with poetry, not with movements of philosophical or religious thought in the nineteenth century. The verse directly produced by the Anglican and Roman Catholic revivals in England is, for the most part, of no more than illustrative interest. I am not attempting to deny merit to the poetry of Keble, Newman, Faber, and the rest. But none of these men will appear to the twentieth-century reader to have been primarily poets. Still less are they central to the subject of this book, the development of the Romantic tradition. Those religious poets of the age who may be so considered worked at a deeper level, where imaginative poetry and mysticism meet. Of the poetry and personality of Robert Stephen Hawker, a somewhat anomalous product of the Anglo-Catholic revival, I have already written, and in a later chapter will have something to say of the two Anglican pre-Raphaelite poets, Christina Rossetti and Richard Watson Dixon. But the three men who most fully exemplify the withdrawal of nineteenth-century Romantic poetry into the region of religious mysticism were all Roman Catholics.

For the first time since the seventeenth century, England produced, in Coventry Patmore, and later in Hopkins and Francis Thompson, three poets who were also Catholic mystics. Their work has an intellectual adventurousness of style which sharply differentiates it from that of their contemporaries and suggests a comparison with Crashaw and the other metaphysical poets.

It is natural to group these three Victorian Roman Catholic poets together. The two younger men each, at different periods, enjoyed the friendship of the older. There are striking differences as well as some parallels between the style of the three. They form a very interesting group, showing the different nature of the stimulus which Roman Catholic mysticism gave to the poetic imagination in their several generations. It is also instructive to note how they form a sort of natural series, running parallel with the development of the Aesthetic Movement which was the main trend of English poetry in the later half of the century. Patmore was the friend first of Tennyson, later of Rossetti; Hopkins of Bridges and Dixon; while one naturally associates Thompson with the little poets of the 'nineties.

Coventry Patmore was born in 1823 at Woodford Green, in Epping Forest. His father, Peter Patmore, had some reputation as a writer, and was an early admirer of Wordsworth. He appears to have been a man of some intelligence, and allowed his son's character to develop freely according to its own bent, though at the age of sixteen he was sent to school in France. The elder Patmore, however, who had been a famous dandy in his youth, made himself unpopular with his contemporaries, first through an unfortunate and fatal duel in which he had been involved, later, in 1854, by the publication of his memoirs, which were accused of bias and inaccuracy. In 1844 he found himself ruined by a speculation in railway shares, and had to quit the country, leaving his son completely penniless. The latter supported himself for two years by doing literary hack-work. His first volume of youthful poems appeared in 1844, and though the reviewer of *Blackwood's* made them the subject of an attack (partly because of the unpopularity of his father, partly because they showed the influence of the "Cockney School" of Keats and Leigh Hunt), were, on the whole, well received. In 1846 the attention of Monckton Milnes was drawn to them, and he secured for Patmore an appointment as a supernumerary assistant in the Department of Printed Books in the British Museum, which post he occupied for the next twenty years. In 1847 occurred his first marriage, to Emily Andrews the daughter of a Nonconformist minister. It was on his courtship of her that the story of *The Angel in the House* was to be based. This extremely happy marriage had a decisive influence on the

9

development of Patmore's thought and poetry, which continued after his wife's death in 1862. During the years of his marriage Patmore supplemented his income by doing work for the literary periodicals, and his house became the centre of a literary circle which included Tennyson, Browning, Carlyle, Ruskin, and the pre-Raphaelites. Shortly after his wife's death he made a visit to Rome, where, largely under the influence of Aubrey de Vere and Manning, he was converted to the Roman Catholic Church. It was here that he met Marianne Byles, a convert of Manning's, who became his second wife. She was possessed of a considerable fortune, and this enabled Patmore to resign his post at the British Museum, and to settle on an estate in Ashdown Forest. Here, in 1868 he issued privately the first odes of the collection later to be known as *The Unknown Eros.* He later settled at Hastings, where, in 1880, his second wife died, and in the following year he married a third time. His last years, till his death in 1896, were spent at Lymington in Hampshire.

It is usual to speak of Tennyson and Browning as the "great" Victorian poets, yet if any poet, between the time of Keats and that of Hopkins, merits that title, I believe, that in spite of his manifest eccentricities and inequalities, it is Coventry Patmore. His work arises from an exalted imaginative vision, which is accompanied by a completely conscious, systematic, and consistent process of intellectualization, and these two elements are held together in a unity of emotion, sensuous experience, and thought. The starting-point of his poetry is Christian theology, combined with the half-Platonic doctrines of Romantic Love. The latter element had been present in English poetry from the Middle Ages downward, but had degenerated into the mere sentimentalism from which he sought to redeem it. Nevertheless, the imaginative experience conveyed by Patmore's poetry is at the same time both intensely personal and universal. The vitality of his thought expresses itself in his great though unequal technical originality and sensitiveness. Moreover, while both Keats and Hopkins died prematurely, with the spiritual and intellectual conflicts of their natures unresolved, Patmore's *Unknown Eros* represents the mature flowering of the poet's talent, at the end of his long life. Such completeness of vision and intellectual integrity are, I suggest, the qualities characteristic of poetry which has universally been accounted great. They are found to a larger degree, it seems to me, in the work of Patmore than in that of Tennyson or Browning, or any other of his contemporaries.

The doctrines of the Roman Catholic Church gave the final impulse to the poetry of Patmore; but the essential qualities of his genius were clearly apparent in his work long before his conversion to Rome. In acclaiming the greatness of *The Unknown Eros* it is possible to under-estimate *The Angel in the House*. The merits of this poem are very con-siderable—indeed, I think it has a certain freshness and charm which are lacking in the later work. The originality, the combination of mysticism and realism, the intellectual alert-ness, the agile play of metaphysical wit which recalls Donne and the seventeenth century generally—all these qualities which place Patmore in a class apart from the rest of his generation—are already fully developed in *The Angel in the House*.

This story of two apparently commonplace middle-class lovers universalizes a portion of the life of its time in the same way as a good novel does, but the verse-form adds a sense of infinity which prose can hardly give. The direct, unforced, yet at the same time sensitive, treatment of contemporary manners is very rare in Victorian poetry. Tennyson attempts it in the prologue to *The Princess* (though only by way of prelude to a fantasy):

> Sir Walter Vivian all a summer's day
> Gave his broad lawns until the set of sun
> Up to the people: thither flocked at noon
> His tenants, wife and child, and thither half
> The neighbouring borough with their Institute

Of which he was the patron. I was there
From college, visiting the son,—the son
A Walter too,—with others of our set,
Five others: we were seven at Vivian place.

And me that morning Walter showed the house,
Greek, set with busts: from vases in the hall
Flowers of all heavens, and lovelier than their names
Grew side by side; and on the pavement lay
Carved stones of the Abbey-ruin in the park,
Huge Ammonites, and the first bones of Time
And on the tables every clime and age
Jumbled together; celts and calumets,
Claymore and snowshoe, toys in lava, fans
Of sandal, amber, ancient rosaries,
Laborious orient ivory sphere in sphere,
The cursed Malayan crease, and battle-clubs
From the isles of palm: and higher on the walls,
Betwixt the monstrous horns of elk and deer,
His own forefathers' arms and armour hung. . . .

These lines, and the pages which follow, are a sort of *tour de force*. But, compare the unstudied naturalness of *The Morning Call* from Patmore's poem:

A voice, the sweeter for the grace
    Of Suddenness, while thus I dream'd,
"Good morning!" said or sang. Her face
    The mirror of the morning seem'd.
Her sisters in the garden walk'd
    And would I come? Across the hall
She took me; and we laughed and talk'd
    About the Flower-show and the Ball.
Their pinks had won a spade for prize;
    But this was gallantly withdrawn
For "Garth on Wiltshire Butterflies!"
    Allusive! So we paced the lawn,
Close-cut, and with geranium plots,
    A rival glow of green and red;
Then counted sixty apricots

On one small tree; the gold-fish fed;
And watch'd where, black with scarlet tans,
Proud Psyche stood and flash'd like flame
Showing and shutting splendid fans;
And in the prize we found its name.

To me it is obvious that there is not only more of real life
in this scene, but also far more poetry than in Tennyson's
lines. The form helps; for these comparatively simple, alter-
nate-rhymed octosyllables carry the reader along, like the
couplets of Chaucer or Crabbe, without effort, over the
homelier passages of narrative, or rise to a lyric intensity, as
the occasion demands. The blank verse which Tennyson
employs, on the other hand was designed for epic; its structure involves such studied involutions of phrase as:

And me that morning Walter showed the house,

and its general movement is rhetorical and heavy. Some of
the lines read like burlesque. Both passages deal with a sophisticated way of life in a society which has since passed away—
but note how Patmore's sense of eternity leads him to select
what is really gracious and valuable in that way of life, while
Tennyson's lines already confront us with something ugly and
absurd in the Victorian bourgeois domestic interior (and
that in no mood of satire)—the monstrous bad taste of the
collection of bric-a-brac—"of every clime and age jumbled
together"—which adorns Sir Walter's hall. There is a patent
touch of snobbery too in Tennyson's whole conception.

Swinburne, and several other contemporaries saw fit to
ridicule and parody the realism of *The Angel in the House*, and
a responsible critic compared Patmore to Tupper. But such
passages as that I have quoted are not flat or prosaic at all.
Patmore's mysticism, his metaphysical sense, gives to the
details of common life a significance which brings them into
proper relation with the more exalted emotions with which
his poetry also deals. Wordsworth's vision lead him to attempt
to establish a similar relation. Sometimes he succeeds—

notably in the description of London in the seventh book of
The Prelude—but at others a certain odd insensitiveness in
his nature gives to his realistic passages a clumsiness which so
often leads to them being ridiculed—sometimes unjustly.
Cowper and Crabbe have the same genius for detailed
domestic genre-painting, but their purpose is moral, not
metaphysical. We have to go back to the Middle Ages, to
Chaucer, to find the same loving and vivid delineation, in
narrative verse, of scenes of contemporary manners. Though
Chaucer is not, like Patmore, a mystic, the spiritual sense and
the wholeness of the culture in which he lived furnished him
with the same intuition of the poetic significance of apparently trivial events. The scenes between Honoria and her
lover in *The Angel in the House* live with the same freshness
as those of the courtship of Troilus in Chaucer's great poem.
In the fourteenth or the nineteenth century, the imagination
of the poet fixes on what is most permanent in human
nature. Each poem seems to us contemporary.

But the central matter of the poem? Patmore's lover is, of
course, so very Victorian; his exalted sentiments are surely a
trifle dated? I would reply that he is no less Victorian than
Chaucer's lovers, with their elaborate ritual of courtship, are
mediæval; Shakespeare's with their braveries and verbal
quibblings, or Sir Philip Sidney with Platonism of the Renaissance; Donne with his "metaphysical" taste for far-fetched
analogies and his introspection of the seventeenth century.
The reality of Love alone remains unchanged; the modes by
which it manifests itself, under different intellectual climates
and social conventions, are infinite. We may or may not be
able to-day to recognize our reactions in those of Patmore's
lover, but we cannot deny the ultimate reality of the poet's
analysis of his state of mind. Patmore's intellect is never
divorced from his emotions or from his physical sensibility.
It is his precise definition of the state of the lover which lifts
his poem above the mawkishness of Tennyson's love-passages
or the crude adolescent fantasies of Swinburne.

The Angel in the House, was inscribed by the author "to the memory of her by whom and for whom I became a poet". Patmore's love for Emily Andrews, who was his first wife, forms the actual basis of the poem. This love was the initial experience from which all his later poetry sprung, and around which his thought, particularly his mystical view of the nature of marriage, crystallized. Long after her death, when Patmore had become a Roman Catholic and had married a second time, he continued to regard his first wife as a saint, although she had had a puritanical hatred and fear of Rome.

The Unknown Eros was first published in its present form in 1877—twenty-three years after the first appearance of *The Angel in the House.* These Odes are therefore the fruit of prolonged and matured meditation, accompanied by a wide reading which included St. Thomas Aquinas, St. Bernard, St. John of the Cross, and among the poets, Crashaw. On a very much smaller scale, they bear somewhat the same relation to the earlier poem as Dante's *Paradiso* does to the *Vita Nuova.* To appraise adequately the beauty and subtlety of the thought enshrined in *The Unknown Eros* would require a far wider knowledge of mystical theology than I can possibly lay claim to. Patmore is deliberately venturing on regions of experience which lay quite outside those in which his contemporaries worked, but the emotional and intellectual integrity of his vision is nevertheless firmly and securely maintained throughout.

The form of those poems is inseparable from their content; it is, technically as adventurous as the thought. The Odes are written in a rhymed free-verse. Historically, this is a logical development from certain seventeenth-century precedents —Patmore mentions the irregular madrigals of Drummond of Hawthornden (based on Italian models) and the wrongly termed "Pindaric" Odes of Cowley and his imitators. But in fact a new type of English verse is here created. Patmore takes his place as one of the few poets of the century since the generation of the Romantics who systematically developed the structure of English versification. In a sense he stands beside Hopkins as one of the originators of the changed attitude to metrical problems which characterizes modern poetry. This, however, has been obscured, since the verse of the twentieth century has chosen, almost exclusively to follow the way of Hopkins, the peculiarities of whose prosody are based on spoken speech, rather than Patmore's extension of Miltonic cadences. It is somewhat disappointing, though not altogether surprising to learn, that, though Patmore was one of the small number of Hopkins's contemporaries who read the latter's poems in manuscript he experienced no sympathy with or understanding of the younger poet's aims. Patmore's *Essay on English Prosody*, should, along with Hopkins's remarks on his own "sprung rhythm", be read by anyone who wishes to gain an idea of the true nature of English verse. Patmore's Essay and Hopkins's Preface contain almost all that has been written on the subject that is of any value whatever. They are supplementary one to another, and taken together, their findings will explain almost all the apparent irregularities to be found in later experiments in "free-verse"—that is, when such experiments have proved their initial success by satisfying the ear. Whereas Hopkins was the first to define clearly the primary importance of the part played by *stress* in English verse, and to show what freedom was possible through the use of shifting stress and by the introduction of variety in the number of unstressed syllables, Patmore emphasizes—what indeed should at all times have been obvious, but which has almost always been ignored by prosodical theorists—the relations of rhythm to actual *time*. He points out that lines of apparently irregular lengths may actually represent time units of equal direction because of the part played by silent pauses both within and at the ends of the lines. If the Essay is carefully studied, after a little thought many problems arising out of traditional English versification will explain themselves.

Whereas *The Angel in the House* tells, after a thinly veiled fashion, the story of Patmore's own courtship of his first wife, *The Unknown Eros* develops the original romantic experience into which the poet was then initiated into a mystical philosophy of married love. For Patmore the Marriage of the Lamb was "more than a metaphor", and the essential androgynous nature of the Man, and the union between God and Man, was revealed in the marriage relationship. This latter theme is particularly worked out in those poems of the series which have the myth of Cupid and Psyche for their subject. The world of these poems, like that of Crashaw and many other mystics, is one where spirit and sense are inextricably mingled. They treat of high matters, which it is not, perhaps, the province of the present essay to deal with in any detail. But interspersed among them are other poems of a plainer nature, some of which, such as *The Azalea*, which deals with the death of the beloved, are of great simplicity and tenderness. Some of these, such as *The Toys* have a homely pathos, which when they are read out of their context, gives them something of an air of sentimentality. Inevitably, the anthologists have seized on these, and by so doing have given rise to an altogether false conception of the nature of Patmore's genius.

I have ventured to suggest a parallel between the development of Patmore and that of Dante, from the *Vita Nuova* to the *Commedia*. In the first we have a more or less straightforward narrative of an early experience of romantic love. In the latter the themes therein enunciated are expanded in the light of a mature religious vision of the universe. The progress of Patmore from *The Angel in the House* to *The Unknown Eros* is, though on a much smaller scale, exactly similar—save that the Odes may be said to constitute a miniature *Paradiso*, the expression of the *Inferno* being wanting in Patmore's poetry. (Perhaps it would not be altogether fanciful to suggest that to find the *Inferno* in Victorian poetry, we must look elsewhere, to the work of other writers—especially to some of those more fully dealt with in other chapters of this book, such as Beddoes and James Thomson.) But Dante's progress from the *Vita Nuova* to the *Commedia* included also his political experience, and his political ideas were organically linked to his vision of romantic love. His bitter condemnation of his opponents, the Papal and anti-Imperial party, breaks out even from the heights of the *Paradiso*. Accordingly, in Patmore's later poems, we also find, among the rest, the political Odes; and here we are brought up against a side of the poet's character very different from that revealed in the rest of his work, and at first sight it is a baffling and repellent side:

> In the year of the great crime,
> When the false English nobles and their Jew
> By God demented, slew
> The Trust they stood twice pledged to keep from wrong,
> One said, Take up thy Song
> That breathes the mild and almost mythic time
> Of England's prime!
> But I, Ah me,
> The freedom of the few
> That, in our free land, were indeed the free
> Can song renew? . . .

What is this "great crime"? In a note as harsh and bitter as the poem itself, Patmore informs us: "In this year the middle and upper classes were disfranchised by Mr. Disraeli's Government, and the final destruction of the liberties of England by the Act of 1884 rendered inevitable." The lines refer to the Reform Bill of 1867. They are only one instance of Patmore's uncompromising hostility to the democratic progress of the century. Not only does he hurl the contemptuous epithet "Jew" at Disraeli, like any modern Fascist, but in another poem there is his characterization of Gladstone:

> His leprosy's so perfect that men call him clean.

Patmore's attitude to the main problems which exercised his age is consistent—and consistently reactionary. Democracy has destroyed the liberties of England, and the future holds only shame and anarchy. Poetry—his poetry—is "a dead language"; he expresses a doubt whether there will be a posterity that cares for letters at all: "Unpalatable and unacceptable as the suggestion may be, it cannot be denied by persons who are able and willing to look facts in the face that there are already strong indications of a relapse into a long-protracted period of social and political disorganization, so complete that there shall be no means of leisure or even living for a learned class, nor any audience for what it has to impart. Such recrudescences of civilization that have occurred, and they may occur again, though the prospect may be as incredible to most Europeans at the present moment as it must have been to the lieges of the Eternal City at the height and sudden turning-point of its popular glory and seemingly consolidated order." Science, in *The Two Deserts*, is dismissed with a faintly supercilious smile:

> Not greatly moved with awe am I
> To learn that we may spy
> Five thousand firmaments beyond our own.
> The best that's known of the heavenly bodies does them credit small.

Who can say that Patmore's pessimism concerning civilization has not been in part justified? Yet it is hard to forgive so embittered a reactionary, who refuses to seek for any solution, or to admit of any hope for mankind as a whole; who sees in the loss of his class's privilege the ruin of his country.

Yet we must reconcile this side of Patmore's character with that of the gentle Romantic lover of *The Angel in the House*, the poet of *The Azalea* and *The Toys*, the quiet meditative singer of *St. Valentine's Day* and *Winter*, the man, infinitely tender, who wrote in *Tristitia:*

> For God is everywhere,
> Go down to deepest Hell, and He is there,

And as a true but quite estranged Friend,
He works, 'gainst gnashing teeth of devilish ire,
With love deep hidden lest it be blasphemed,
If possible, to blend
Ease with the pangs of its inveterate fire;
Yea, in the worst
And from His Face most wilfully accursed
Of souls in vain redeem'd
He does with potions of oblivion kill
Remorse of the lost Love that helps them still.

Nor was Patmore's interpretation of Catholic doctrine narrow or bigoted. We are told that he declared that the Greek sculptors, the poets of the Renaissance, and even Crébillon *fils* were all Catholic in their way—an intellectual liberalism which Hopkins looked upon with suspicion.[1] Nevertheless in embracing the tenets of the Roman Church, he committed himself to an alliance with a body which was in conflict at many points with what we can only regard as the progressive forces of the age. James Thomson, abandoning himself to the utter despair of *The City of Dreadful Night*, still managed to remain, in Chesterton's phrase, "democratic in the dark". Catholicism provided Patmore with the body of intellectual convictions and imaginative images, which enabled him, as I believe, to rise to heights unattained by any other poet of his generation. But this was at the price of that bitterness and isolation from the main currents of the time which breaks out in the solitary impotence of the political Odes.

Gerard Manley Hopkins, the Jesuit priest, was a born revolutionary. It would be interesting—but quite unprofitable—to speculate as to what might have been his destiny, if instead of following the course he did, he had joined with the fighting Socialists of his day. Certain passages in his letters, and his poem *Tom's Garland* (on the unemployed) show how

[1] *Derek Patmore:* Introduction to *Selected Poems of Coventry Patmore.*

clearly and unflinchingly he estimated what was the real condition of the working class in his time:

> Tom—garlanded with squat and surly steel
> Tom; then Tom's fallowbootfellow piles pick
> By him and rips out rockfire homeforth—sturdy Dick;
> Tom Heart-at-Ease, Tom Navvy: he is all for his meal
> Sure, 's bed now. Low be it: lustily he his low lot (feel
> That ne'er need hunger, Tom; Tom seldom sick,
> Seldomer hearthsore; that treads through, prickproof, thick
> Thousands of thorns, thoughts) swings though, Commonweal
> Little I reck ho! lacklevel in, if all had bread:
> What! Country is honour enough in all us—lordly head,
> With heaven's lights high hung round, or, mother-ground
> That mammocks, mighty foot. But no way sped,
> Nor mind nor mainstrength; gold go garlanded
> With, perilous, O nó; nor yet plod safe shod sound;
> Undenizened, beyond bound
> Of earth's glory, earth's ease, all; no one, nowhere,
> In wide the world's weal; rare gold, bold steel, bare
> In both; care, but share care—
> This, by Despair, bred Hangdog dull; by rage,
> Manwolf, worse; and their packs infest the age.

It is such things as this that make us feel Hopkins to belong essentially to our own time.

But the struggle revealed in Hopkins's poetry is a spiritual civil war, fought out within his own soul; and the revolution which he initated in the style of English verse is that outward expression of that internal conflict. His poems are so different in manner from all other Victorian verse, that it would, it seems, have been impossible to publish them during his lifetime (but it is not easy for one of my generation to think charitably of Bridges's suppression of them, or of the apologetic manner in which he finally introduced them to the world). No poet possessed a more astonishing sensibility to the nature of his medium. Ultimately, it is not so much the technical innovations—"sprung rhythm", the use of alliteration and internal rhyme etc.—which give to his verse its peculiar quality, but his miraculous sense of rhythm, of pause, and vowel and consonant harmony. To these must be added the sharpness and freshness of his physical sensibility—especially to natural beauty. He prunes away ruthlessly the growth of verbiage which had sapped the vitality of the language of Victorian poetry, and gives us living speech stripped to its essentials. Hopkins's obscurity and apparent eccentricities of manner are, in their nature, the very reverse of Browning's.[1] Those of the latter poet arise from an attempt to force the verse and a mode of thought which is naturally alien to it together in a factitious unity. In Hopkins the form and the thought are absolutely *one*. There is no unusual construction or apparent breach of the rules of syntax which is not the logical development of some principle already implicit in living idiomatic English. The combination of the principles of stress, alliteration, and quantity, which go to make up the style of Hopkins's verse, is, fundamentally the same as had existed in Old English Poetry before the essential genius of the language had been overlaid by French influence.

Finally, Hopkins's verse always justified itself when read aloud. There is only one other poet of the period who forged a style in some respects similar. Doughty resembles Hopkins in the freshness of his physical sensibility, in the wholly native character of his rhythm and syntax, and in his exploitation of heavy stresses and deep pauses. But his aim was to create an epic style, while Hopkins's is subjective and lyrical.

All Hopkins's poetry, except for *Juvenilia*, takes its rise from his religious experiences—that "naked encounter of sensualism and asceticism" which shocked the timid Bridges. The poems of his Oxford days—the period of his conversion —such as *Heaven Haven*—have a limpid, untroubled beauty.

---

[1] It is worth noting, however, that both Hopkins and Browning were close students of Greek poetry; and it is possible that a reading of Aeschylus' choruses, with his characteristic verbal daring, may have brought the same influence to bear on the work of the two English poets.

They are of the calm before the storm, and show how sweet must have been the initial experience which was to prelude so intense a struggle:

> And I have asked to be
> Where no storms come,
> Where the green swell is in the havens dumb,
> And out of the swing of the sea.

After he had taken orders, there followed a self-imposed silence of some years—broken at last by the magnificent *Wreck of the Deutschland*—a poem epic in spirit, if not in form. In the work of his middle period, however, the leading theme is provided by Hopkins's sensibility to natural and to human beauty—a sensibility which is as acute as Keats's, and more directly physical:

> . . . beauty-in-the-ghost, deliver it, early now,
> long before death
> Give beauty back, beauty, beauty, beauty, back to God,
> beauty's self and beauty's giver.

—this is the gesture of sublimation which Hopkins is continually making. Yet in the final Sonnets—*"Thou art indeed just Lord, if I contend"*, *Carrion Comfort*, *"I wake and feel the fell of dark"*, and the rest—above all *"No worst, there is none"*—we see how terrible for him the internal conflict had become. He reasons passionately with himself or with his God; he maps the mountains of the mind—

> . . . . cliffs of fall
> Frightful sheer, no man fathomed. Hold them cheap
> May who ne'er hung there. . . .

and approaches a pit of despair more profound than that opened up by the intellectual doubt that dogged his contemporaries, or the mere nightmare life-in-death that James Thomson endured. We must return to *Samson Agonistes* for a parallel.

Patmore's religious faith, except when he turns his eyes outward to the world, and gives vent to the bitterness of the political Odes, enabled him to move in a paradisal region of intellectual light and love, unapproached by his contemporaries. For Hopkins, of a younger generation, and with senses —intellectual and physical—so acutely awake that he seems to us to belong to no past age, but for each of us who read him to-day contemporary, there could be no such refuge. The metaphysic of Catholicism gives to his verse its living and intellectually organic quality. But the conflict set up between the intense vitality of his senses and the ascetic modes of thought he adopted remained unresolved at the date of his early death. Only in some of the *Holy Sonnets* of Donne, written at the time where the thought of the Middle Ages was being superseded by the modern empirical method, do we find a similar conflict expressed—but in Hopkins, I think, the struggle is fiercer, the suffering more bitter: it would be almost outside the power of words to express, if it were not for his nearly superhuman command of language.

Now that we have the poems of Hopkins, it is difficult to echo the chorus of praise with which, round about the turn of the century, the work of Francis Thompson was acclaimed. The two poets deal with almost identical spiritual experiences, and from the same standpoint of Catholic mysticism, but Thompson's verse appears meretricious, and fails in every respect when compared with Hopkins's. The power of the latter lies in his absolute economy of language, which rather throws into relief than detracts from the strength of his acute physical sensibility. Thompson's verse is not only overloaded with sensuous imagery, but at the same time weakened by diffuseness. *The Hound of Heaven* does indeed succeed in convincing us of the reality of the experience behind it, but its floridity, the artificial nature of its diction, and the remote character of its images are sad encumbrances. If we compare it with any single one of the great sonnets of Hopkins, the whole complicated structure of Thompson's

ode falls to the ground. If this is true of his most ambitious
poem, it is still more so of the rest of his work, which, except
for the admirably direct lines, *In no Strange Land*, reveals
itself as a mere decorative piling-up of verbal effects.

The spiritual ardours of Patmore and Hopkins give to
their work a genuine kinship with that of the seventeenth-
century metaphysicals. With Thompson, on the other hand,
the resemblance is superficial. His affectation of the baroque
is mainly an archaic mannerism, and his real affinities are
with the poets of the Aesthetic Movement, and with Shelley;
in his work the faults of the latter poet—diffuseness, intellectual impreciseness, the want of a sense of common reality,
the excessive predominance of sound over sense—run to
seed. In his diction a tendency we detect in nineteenth-
century verse from Tennyson to the pre-Raphaelites is
pushed to its furthest point. The language becomes stilted
and unreal—not only remote from the spoken speech, but
from the natural genius of the language itself. It is here that
the contrast with Hopkins is most striking. The compounds
and new formations employed by the latter are always purely
English in their character; the basis of his diction is formed
by short, simple, and colloquial words, and the rhythms of his
verse are a logical development of those of the spoken
language. Such a poem as Thompson's *A Corymbus for
Autumn*, on the other hand, is a mere cluster of forced rhymes,
unnatural constructions, latinisms like "impurpurate",
"rubiginous", "illuminous", "conflagrate", Wardour Street
words, and *clichés* too reminiscent of Keats's over-lushness—
"overshaden", "enclip", "globed clusters", "wassailous",
"viewlessly",—and Swinburne-Shelley vague magnilo-
quences—"untameable feet". The whole is almost devoid of
meaning.

Thompson's undisciplined flamboyance in the choice of
words and his fondness for complicated, unnatural rhymes
may be symptoms induced by his addiction to opium. There
is an atmosphere of unreality, of escape into a dream-world

of glittering colours and tinkling sounds about his poetry, which we may attribute to the same cause. It is impossible to doubt the reality of the central religious experience—at any rate in *The Hound of Heaven*—but this vision is weakened and clouded in the narcotic dreams of an escapist.

Thompson appears to have been a weak and feckless creature—if also a charming and childlike one—a very different type of man from the ascetic Hopkins. His religious poetry makes slight demands on the intellectual capacity of his readers, but offers an exciting and sensuous ritual; it is these qualities, I am afraid, which have contributed to its wide popularity with the public as a whole.

I am not forgetting Thompson's sufferings. He knew the depths of destitution in the streets of London. The unearthly, ideal quality of his verse gains a good deal when we contrast it with the darkness of the poet's personal story—up to the time he was rescued and reclaimed by the Meynells. His history, like that of Chatterton or De Quincey, has something of the poignancy of myth—he is the Vagabond Poet. But this is sheer sentimentality—an insult in fact to his real sufferings. He was a remarkable and unlikely phenomenon, but serious criticism cannot for a moment contend that he was a good poet. His near-namesake, James Thomson, whose fate was not altogether dissimilar, pursued a longer and a lonelier course of despair, and found none to befriend him at the end. In his case, there was no gleam of religious faith to sustain him, yet he came nearer, much nearer, to transmuting his despair into the spiritual material of true poetry.

I have suggested that in the confused intellectual atmosphere of the Victorian Age, when a narrow sciential materialism challenged the validity of so much which the imagination affirmed, the Roman Church, preserving elements of an older and more comprehensive intellectual culture, offered a refuge. To poets especially, it furnished elements upon which their imagination might freely work—but at the price of isolation from the main intellectual currents of the age. By taking the path of mysticism Patmore attained the poetic heights of *The Unknown Eros.* In Hopkins an internal conflict of such intensity was set up, that we may believe that it was actually among the causes of his premature death; but his poetry achieves an intellectual and formal vitality which lifts it far above that of his contemporaries. In the generation of Thompson, the same tradition of Roman Catholic mysticism had become the refuge of a weakling, and the sublime visions it furnished mingled with those artificially produced by opium. Only from a synthesis, wherein the mind's imaginative perceptions both of the spiritual and material worlds are combined, can great poetry arise.

Chapter 5

PRE-RAPHAELITISM AND THE AESTHETIC WITHDRAWAL

IN the verse of the generation of Tennyson and Browning
we see a conscious attempt to deliver a "message" and to
assimilate the new material presented to the imagination
by the changed additions of life in the nineteenth century,
and, persisting along with this, but not organically fused
with it, images inherited from the Romantic tradition.
Nevertheless, both Tennyson and Browning, in fact, write
most happily when they are least disturbed by their consciousness of a duty to teach or to demonstrate a psychological—i.e. a scientific—truth. The purely decorative parts
of the *Idylls of the King*, the opening of *The Lotos Eaters*, *The
Lady of Shalott*, *Mariana*—all of them essentially paintings
in words or pieces of lovely tapestry—these are the poems of
Tennyson which give the most complete artistic satisfaction.
Likewise, much of the best of Browning's work has the
character of historical vignettes. The classical *Artemis
Prologises* is an example. *The Bishop Orders his Tomb* and *My
Last Duchess* have a psychological motive, though only a
slight one; but it is the décor of these poems—capturing so
well the Renaissance love of luxury and fantastic ornament—
that renders them memorable. Among his poems of contemporary life, *Meeting at Night* and *Parting at Morning*
have the same completeness and are likewise devoid of any
direct didactic intention.

In the second half of the century the general tendency of
English poetry was to abandon the attempt either to deal with
the external world, or to express any "philosophy". The poets
withdrew into the contemplation of purely decorative
beauty. This movement, in England, had two phases. The
first and most important was the pre-Raphaelite movement

which took shape in the 'fifties, and which had spent its force by the middle of the 'eighties. It was a movement which primarily affected painting and the arts of decoration, but also found its expression in the sphere of poetry. If its products look dated to-day, it is well to remember the massed forces of Victorian middle-class Philistinism with which the pre-Raphaelites had to contend. A real insistence on purely aesthetic values was necessary, and it is to the pre-Raphaelites's credit that this reform was to a large extent effected. The name of the "Aesthetic Movement" is generally restricted to the literature and art of the 'nineties. But in the field of poetry this was essentially a resumption of pre-Raphaelitism. The movement had now acquired a sort of metaphysic, though its sources were diverse, its development complex, and its genealogy hard to trace. Matthew Arnold, with his gospel of "Culture", and Ruskin may to some extent be regarded as its prophets and forerunners. But both of these men were essentially Puritans, by upbringing and by temperament. Ruskin had tended to identify moral and aesthetic values, but the latter, for him, arose out of a consideration of the former. But the real philosopher of the later Aesthetic Movement was Pater, whose thought combined elements of German aesthetic Hellenism with a religiosity whose source must be looked for in the "ritualist" tendency which had followed up the Oxford Movement, and which had affinities, also, with the aesthetic Catholicism of Chateaubriand. But above all, for Pater, moral considerations disappear; the moment of aesthetic experience becomes the sole significant reality.

In the poetry of the 'nineties there was some infiltration of French influence—mainly that of Baudelaire and Verlaine —but it operated, for the most part, on a superficial level. The first poem of Verlaine to appear in English version was one translated by Arthur O'Shaughnessy. This Irish poet, himself, was essentially a pre-Raphaelite, with a touch of the traditional nineteenth-century Irish style of Moore and

Mangan added. Arthur Symons was perhaps the most intelli-
gent of the poetic *entrepreneurs* between England and France,
and his *Symbolist Movement* still remains an excellent critical
introduction to its subject. His own verse is very unequal.
Some of the best of it illustrates the influence of contemporary movements of painting, such as the work of Whistler,
and later, Sickert, on the poetry of the period. Another poet,
Eugene Lee Hamilton, probably came nearest to assimilating
his Continental models. Lee Hamilton, though he finally
recovered his health and entered upon a new, happily
married life, was, for a number of years, a total invalid. He
suffered from a cerebro-spinal disease which forced him to lie
supine, helpless, and bedridden. In this condition he wrote,
or more often, painfully and slowly dictated, his *Imaginary
Sonnets*. They have a touch of the pessimism of Leopardi, and
also of Heine, whose fate, in his later years, had been similar to Lee Hamilton's, but the main influence is that of
Baudelaire and the French Parnassians. These poems, though
sometimes the note is forced, have a certain hard and
sterile perfection of style, which is in keeping, with the
circumstances of their composition.

But in the most typical poets of the time, English Romantic
influences, and above all that of the pre-Raphaelites, really
form the basis of their style. Within the narrow limits in
which these poets chose to work, Dowson came nearest to
success—but that is not very near. He survives, in a shadowy
way, through the charm of, at most, two or three minor
poems. The much inferior Lionel Johnson, whom it is
customary to name with him, is remembered for two poems
—*The Dark Angel* and *On The Statue of Charles I*. And they
are poor enough, wordy, unequal, and rhetorical in manner.
How strange that this poet was once actually praised for his
"Latin" precision! For it is the great condemnation of these
poets that they notably failed to achieve the perfection of
style at which they aimed. Their imagery is trite, their
technique inadequate, and their diction vague, diffuse, and

lifeless. They exist in a kind of half-world, on the fringes of literary history, and are of more interest to the social historian than to the critic. Their lives were commonly wretched; those who did not die young outlived their talents and their reputations. There was a good deal of posturing, by way of protest against the moral Philistinism of the bourgeois, and some scandal. There were a number of melodramatic repentances, and doubtless sincere, but hardly profound, conversions to Roman Catholicism. The unhappy fate of Oscar Wilde gives to his story an illustrative value in relation to the atmosphere of the time; his writings (of which the least important are his poems) reveal a second-rate, superficially brilliant mind, with a great capacity for assimilating and vulgarizing diverse, though often excellent models. All in all, the 'nineties represent a backwater in the history of English poetry. The consideration of that backwater is hardly germane to the main subject of this book.

To both these movements, the pre-Raphaelites, and that of the 'nineties, the general term "Aesthetic" may conveniently be applied—though properly it belongs only to the latter. These trends offer certain analogies with the Symbolist Movement, more or less contemporary with them, which originated in France with Baudelaire, though the formula "art for art's sake" was coined by Gautier, and accepted by the Parnassian poets in France, as well as by the Symbolists. It is instructive to compare the poetry of the Symbolists and that of the pre-Raphaelites and their successors. One cannot consider the work of the latter without reference to the painting of Rossetti, Morris, and Burne-Jones, while a major inspiration of the Symbolists was the music of Wagner. Now painting—as understood in the nineteenth century—is the more decorative, music the more abstract, art. The more intellectual character of the French genius is seen even in this poetry of withdrawal, and Symbolist work tended to be increasingly metaphysical in its preoccupations.

It is fashionable to dismiss these two parallel movements

in English and French poetry as decadent and escapist, with the implication that the poets should have resisted the temptation to withdraw from reality, and have evolved a style of verse capable of dealing adequately with the social problems of the day. But this, for most of them, would have been impossible. The changes going on in the social structure were too rapid, and the answers which the science offered to the questioning mind too uncertain and conflicting to provide an adequate metaphysical structure upon which the poets could have based their criticism of life. Yet, for most of them, the foundations of traditional faith, which had sanctioned a more imaginative vision of the world, seemed irreparably shaken. In these circumstances the only course for the artist who sought to retain his integrity was a withdrawal from the confused and unintelligible reality which lay without. The subjectively apprehended reality of aesthetic experience could at least not be explained away by science. By concentrating upon this, a coherent vision might yet be attained.

But this course was followed with greater consistency by the more intellectual poets of France. They lived in a country more acutely (or at least more openly) disturbed by social change than that of their English contemporaries, in their relatively sheltered and prosperous middle-class security. When the Symbolists entered their Otherworld of pure Art, they did not abandon all attempt to fuse intellectual thought with their imaginative vision. Baudelaire's *Fleurs du Mal*, though his satanism is partly a pose, does represent an attempt, only half-consciously carried out, to explore the metaphysical nature of evil, through the medium of the senses. Rimbaud went further and attempted to pass beyond Good and Evil. Mallarmé is of all the group the most withdrawn from common experience, but he is also the most intensely intellectual. His poetry deals with a very restricted and remote part of reality, yet the tract of feeling dealt with in his poems forms an integral portion of the great whole of possible human experience, and the poet is making a genuine philosophical attempt to explore it. The acrid satirical poetry of Corbière and Laforgue, though apparently only exposing a state of futility, is, fundamentally, an attempt to measure the confusion of external reality against the aesthetic standards that Symbolist poetry had begun to rediscover. It foreshadows the time when poetry can once more be integrated with the exterior world. The outcome of this metaphysical courage of the French poets is a far greater originality, precision, and freedom of style than is to be found in their English contemporaries. Despite the suspicious attitude of the critics, the best of the poetry of the French Symbolists retains vital qualities which recommend it to modern readers. Such qualities are hardly to be found in any of the English pre-Raphaelite and Aesthetic poets before the time of Yeats.

In painting, and also in poetry, the overt aim of the pre-Raphaelites was—as with the first Romantics—a "return to nature", in all her simplicity. They aimed at precision of detail, and indeed, many of the longer narrative poems of Rossetti are difficult to read because the succession of minutely observed natural details distracts from the apprehension of the subject-matter as a whole. Another characteristic of the pre-Raphaelites—that which the name of the group denotes—is their preference for mediæval subject-matter, and their revival of mediæval metrical and literary forms. A sympathy with the older literature, involving its more or less close imitation, had formed an integral part of Romanticism from Chatterton and the "Gothic" writers of the eighteenth century downwards. Such poems as those of Chatterton, Coleridge's *Christabel*, and Keats's *Eve of St. Mark's* in particular, furnished models for the pre-Raphaelites, in its decorative treatment of mediæval scenes. Historical scholarship and the criticism of Ruskin had now revealed a much clearer picture of mediæval civilization, and the excellence of its art; the traditional view of the Renaissance Humanists and the men of the Age of Reason that the Middle

Ages had been wholly a period of Gothic barbarism and monkish superstition was no longer tenable. Nor could the sentimentalized picture of feudalism and chivalry furnished by Scott's novels or even Tennyson's *Idylls of the King* wholly satisfy readers any longer.

But the pre-Raphaelites did not altogether succeed in piercing through to the life of earlier ages. While they employed the religious and other symbols of the old poetry, they rejected the faith which had given these symbols relevance. Hence their work is often at the same time both sentimental and vulgar, lifeless and unreal.

That this is so will become apparent if we analyse intellectually that most typically pre-Raphaelite poem, Rossetti's *The Blessed Damozel*. The heroine—the poet's dead mistress —is represented as in Heaven. But instead of enjoying her felicity, she continually awaits the time when her lover will be reunited to her. Seeing a flight of angels approaching, she expects the event,

> . . . but soon their path
> Was vague in distant spheres:
> And then she cast her arms along
> The golden barriers,
> And laid her face between her hands,
> And wept. (I heard her tears).

But if we take it at its face value, the whole conception is cheaply sentimental and muddled to the point of absurdity. For by any definition of bliss it is impossible to suppose a soul in heaven capable of the emotions in which the Blessed Damozel is represented as indulging. And by the standards of mediæval theology—which the whole framework of the poem implies—her longing for her earthly lover, to the exclusion of her joy in the contemplation of God, is as much a sin—a thing impossible in a redeemed soul—as the excessive grief for the dead of which the poet is himself guilty. The poem was written by Rossetti in his very early years, but it seems almost prophetic of the state of mind which was to be actually his, many years later, after the death of Elizabeth Siddal. The story of how he buried the manuscripts of his poems with her in her coffin, and was then persuaded to make nonsense of this romantic gesture by allowing them to be exhumed, is pathetic, appalling, and not a little nauseating. It bears the same sort of witness as does *The Blessed Damozel* itself to the atmosphere of unreasoned, muddled, romantic sentiment in which Rossetti's passion exercised itself.

In mediæval poetry, the dead always exhort the living to lay aside grief, remembering that those they have loved are in the hands of God. So speaks the voice from the Unquiet Grave in the old ballad, the dead child in the fourteenth-century allegory of *The Pearl*, the Laura of Petrarch's devotion:

> Di me non pianger tu; ch'e' miei di fersi,
> morendo, eterni; e nell' eterno lume,
> quando mostrai di chiudar, gli occhi apersi.

Perhaps this quiet voice cannot satisfy the restless and passionate mind of man. We are troubled when we try to imagine what place the individual human affections ultimately take beneath the light of eternity. The problem exists for all who think and feel intensely, whether they accept the myth of survival after death as objectively true or not. Patmore also, with his intense intellectual faith, in *Tristitia* explores the possibility that the Blessed may grieve for those they have loved on earth—not indeed from a temporary sense of separation, but if the latter should be eternally exiled from Heaven. For Patmore this bare possibility is an awful mystery, hardly to be thought of or expressed in words; a contradiction of the order of things, which will react terribly upon the damned soul who has been its cause. The distance between Patmore's sensitive Ode, and Rossetti's decorative and overloaded poem, measures the distance between the metaphysical and the merely sentimental treatment of love.

Judged by the standards I have suggested above, *The Blessed Damozel* must simply be dismissed as a sentimental and silly poem. There is, however, another line of approach, which may help us to a more sympathetic understanding of this and of the rest of Rossetti's work. The world of this poetry is a kind of limbo, a half-sensuous, pagan dream-world, such as was explored by Edgar Allan Poe, and sometimes, by Shelley. The Christian imagery, derived from Dante and the other early Italian poets, is used merely decoratively and is not really of a piece with this world. Rossetti is an explorer of the subconscious, of subtle states of mind between waking and sleeping:

> There the dreams are multitudes:
>   Some that will not wait for sleep.
> Deep within the August woods;
> Some that hum while rest may steep
>   Weary labour laid a-heap;
>   Interludes,
> Some, grievous moods that weep.
>
> Poets' fancies all are there:
>   There the elf-girls flood with wings
> Vallies full of plaintive air;
>   There breath perfumes; there in rings
>   Whirl the foam-bewildered springs;
>   Siren there
> Winds her dizzy hair and sings.

In his last years Rossetti was a scarcely sane man. And to this period belongs his fragmentary prose tale, *The Orchard Pit*, telling of a strange Siren dwelling in an apple-tree, who lured men to their doom. This is perhaps Rossetti's most intensely imagined work, and the unfinished lyric which forms part of it, well presents the state of Death-in-Life to which his exploration of the dream-world finally lead him:

Piled deep below the screening apple-branch
    They lie with bitter apples in their hands:
And some are only ancient bones that blanch,
And some had ships that last year's wind did launch,
    And some were yesterday the lords of lands.

In the soft dell, among the apple-trees,
    High up above the hidden pit she stands,
And there for ever sings, who gave to these,
That lie below, her magic hour of ease,
    And those her apples holden in their hands.

This in my dreams is shown me; and her hair
    Crosses my lips and draws my burning breath;
Her song spreads golden wings upon the air,
Life's eyes are gleaming from her forehead fair,
    And from her breasts the ravishing eyes of Death.

Men say to me that sleep hath many dreams,
    Yet I knew never but this dream alone:
There, from a dried-up channel, once the stream's,
The glen slopes up; even such in sleep it seems
    As in my waking sight the place well-known.

.   .   .   .   .

My love I call her, and she loves me well:
    But I love her as in the maelstrom's cup
The whirled stone loves the leaf inseparable
That clings to it round all the circling swell,
    And that the same last eddy swallows up.

It is this kind of dream-poetry, rather than the formal peculiarities of their style, or their mediævalism, which is, I think, really characteristic of the pre-Raphaelites. In a sense their movement may be regarded as a resumption of the romantic impulse from the point it had reached in the dream-poetry of Hood, and Darley, which I have already dealt with. But in the poetry of the pre-Raphaelites it has more the quality of reverie. Their very insistence upon visual exactness in their imagery gives to their work a kind of detachment and remoteness. We seem to be gazing at something a

long way off, as through the wrong end of a telescope—
something, too, which is at a great distance in time, as well
as in space. The sense of urgency, of relevancy to the waking
world is gone. The symbols (the poem quoted above is perhaps an exception) seem to be robbed of their significance.

In some respects *The House of Life* contains the most satis-
factory of Rossetti's work. His familiarity with the early
Italian poets gave him an insight into the true nature of the
sonnet form. Milton, in whose hands "the thing became a
trumpet", and Wordsworth, following his example, by
obscuring the outlines of its internal structure and its original
lyrical character, had tended to make the sonnet too much a
vehicle for rhetorical declamation, and furnished dangerous
models for later English poets. The essential balanced
structure and formal development of the sonnet are restored
by Rossetti, and it again becomes a species of poem in which
form and thought develop logically together. Nevertheless,
an undisciplined, rootless man like Rossetti was incapable of
attaining the crystalline clarity and perfect balance of his
models. His archaic and affected diction, the movement of
his lines, clogged with lifeless monosyllables, the vagueness of
his sensuous images—all these tend to blur his picture, and
make his passion seem strained and unreal. His true merit
lies less in direct expressive power, than in his gift for evoking
transient and half-defined states of feeling. This is seen sometimes in the sonnets of *The House of Life*, more frequently in
the songs that are contained in the same work—notably in
the well-known *Wood-spurge*, and *Sudden Light*:

> I have been here before,
>   But when or how I cannot tell:
> I know the grass beyond the door,
>   The sweet keen smell,
> The sighing sound, the lights around the shore.

In poems such as these Rossetti captures a delicate subtlety
of emotion, rather in the manner later brought to perfection

by Walter De la Mare. (The latter, a minor poet of our own time, might almost be called the last representative of the pre-Raphaelite "Renaissance of Wonder".) This visionary quality of Rossetti, both as poet and painter, gives him an affinity with Blake, whose merits he was one of the first to discover. Yet he lacks Blake's essential religious vision, and with it the lyrical intensity, clarity, and freshness which Blake, at any rate in his purely poetical, as distinct from his "prophetic" work, achieves. Rossetti's vision is blurred, lacking any unifying principle. He moves unhappily in a world of dream-symbols, and the weary, clogged rhythms of his verse indicate how imperfectly they are imaginatively apprehended.

It is a relief to turn from Rossetti's poems to those of his sister Christina. She has all the qualities which he lacks—restraint, poise, lightness of touch, a feeling for clean, bright colour. These features arise, no doubt, from her own temperament—a personality more finely constituted than her brother's, for which suffering provided a discipline, and religion an intelligible pattern by which life might be ruled. It is true that her religion—a High Anglican piety—when it impinges directly upon her poetry, produces a certain chill, as it seems to have narrowed and frustrated her emotional life. She rejected two suitors, apparently because she doubted the stability of their religious views. Quite possibly some deeper-seated psychological twist in her emotional nature prompted her to make this rejection. It is obvious from her poetry that it caused her profound suffering. In poem after poem we find this rejection symbolized—the heroine is cheated of her lover by a jealous sister (in whom we may see perhaps Christina's own "super-ego" personified?) or she is snatched from his arms by a mysterious demon, the "Love from the North". Again, in *The Prince's Progress*, the princess dies unwedded, because the prince has delayed too long in crossing the desert to find her. Nevertheless, some of her religious verse is, in its kind, often admirable—note particularly the fine economy and dramatic movement of *The Three*

Enemies, in which the resolved soul resists the temptations, progressively more insidious, of the Flesh, the World, and the Devil:

THE FLESH

"Sweet, thou art pale."
                    "More pale to see,
Christ hung upon the cruel tree
    And bore his father's wrath for me."

"Sweet thou art sad."
                    "Beneath a rod
More heavy, Christ for my sake trod
The winepress of the wrath of God."

"Sweet thou art weary."
                    "Not so Christ:
Whose mighty love for me sufficed
For strength, Salvation, Eucharist."

"Sweet, thou art footsore."
                    "If I bleed,
His feet have bled: yea, in my need
His heart once bled for mine indeed."

THE WORLD

"Sweet, thou art young."
                    "So He was young
Who for my sake in silence hung
Upon the Cross with Passion wrung."

"Look, thou art fair."
                    "He was more fair
Than men, who deigned for me to wear
A visage marred beyond compare."

"And thou hast riches."
                    "Daily bread:
All else is His; Who living, dead,
For me lacked where to lay His head."

"And life is sweet."
                    "It was not so
To Him, Whose Cup did overflow
With mine inutterable woe."

THE DEVIL

"Thou drinkest deep."
                    "When Christ would sup
He drained the dregs from out my cup:
So how should I be lifted up?"

"Thou shalt win glory."
                    "In the skies,
Lord Jesus, cover up mine eyes
Lest they should look on vanities."

"Thou shalt have Knowledge."
                    "Helpless dust!
In Thee, O Lord, I put my trust:
Answer Thou for me, Wise and Just."

"And Might."—
                    "Get thee behind me. Lord,
Who hast redeemed and not abhorred
My soul, oh keep it by Thy Word."

But when she allows her imagination free play in spheres of feeling not directly affected by her piety, the basic religious instinct lying behind the work gives to it a clarity and an inner logic of design not to be found in that of her agnostic brother. Let us take, for example, her best-known narrative poem, *Goblin Market*. This is not directly a religious poem. Laura, the younger of two sisters, is tempted by the powers of evil, the Goblins, and tastes their forbidden fruit. As a result, she pines away, almost to the point of death. Having once savoured its sweetness, she is filled with an overpowering longing to do so again, but no person may a second time meet with the goblin merchants—this is a most accurate psychological description of the nature of sensual sin. The elder sister,

Lizzie, saves Laura by her self-sacrifice, herself braving the dangers of the goblins' glen. She demands to buy the goblins wares, but will not herself taste of them. They try to force her, pressing the fruit upon her mouth and face, and because of this, she is able to carry some of the juices of the fruit back to Laura, who recovers when she has tasted them. The whole story might be read as an allegory of the Fall and Redemption of Man, represented by Laura, the action of the elder sister being analogous to the guiltless self-sacrifice of Christ. There is even, perhaps, a suggestion of the Eucharist in Lizzie's words to Laura on her return:

> She cried "Laura," up the garden,
> "Did you miss me?
> Come and kiss me.
> Never mind my bruises,
> Hug me, kiss me, suck my juices
> Squeezed from goblin fruits for you,
> Goblin pulp and goblin dew.
> Eat me, drink me, love me;
> Laura, make much of me:
> For your sake I have braved the glen
> And had to do with goblin merchant men."

But there is no need to suppose that Christina Rossetti consciously, or even unconsciously, intended this. Lizzie, giving herself for the one she loves, may be taken as a type of the Christian as well as of Christ. The point to note is that the central Christian doctrines of guilt, self-sacrifice, and substitution inform the whole poem, giving significance to what seems at first sight no more than a dream-fantasy or a pastiche of folk-tale.

As a pre-Raphaelite, Christina Rossetti, like Dante Gabriel Rossetti and Morris, creates for herself an artificial dream-world by re-evoking the poetic forms of older romance. But, within its smaller compass, her world has more of the genuine life of the world of romance and folk-tale than theirs. Dante Gabriel Rossetti's ballads—*The White Ship, Eden*

Bower and the rest—especially *Sister Helen*—are exciting enough, but they will not bear comparison with the genuine old ballads. There is much of melodrama about them; their effects are too obviously laboured, the refrains over-artfully introduced. Christina Rossetti's *Sister Maude*—short as it is —comes much nearer to the genuine spirit of the traditional ballads, and to this is added a peculiar personal poignancy of emotion. Simple though it appears, this is one of the poems which, as I have already suggested, may be interpreted in the light of modern psychology. It is the retort of the imaginative, emotional side of Christina Rossetti's nature upon the narrowly pious super-ego which thwarted her:

> Who told my mother of my shame,
>> Who told my father of my dear?
> Oh who but Maude, my sister Maude,
>> Who lurked to spy and peer.
>
> Cold he lies, as cold as stone,
>> With his clotted curls about his face:
> The comeliest corpse in all the world,
>> And worthy of a queen's embrace.
>
> You might have spared his soul, sister,
>> Have spared my soul, your own soul too;
> Though I had not been born at all,
>> He'd never have looked at you.
>
> My father may sleep in Paradise,
>> My mother at Heaven-gate;
> But sister Maude shall get no sleep
>> Either early or late.
>
> My father may wear a golden gown,
>> My mother a crown may win;
> If my dear and I knocked at Heaven-gate
>> Perhaps they'd let us in:
> Not sister Maude, oh sister Maude,
>> Bide *you* with death and sin.

The autumnal languor of pre-Raphaelite poetry—the slow lines with their weary monosyllables, the faint colours, the indirectness of emotional expression—symptomatic of a late phase of Romanticism, and contrasting so strangely with that of the mediæval writers which are the poets' models—is not to be found in Christina Rossetti. Her best work has a lilting, lyrical movement and an April freshness of imagery:

> Long ago and long ago,
>   And long ago still,
> There dwelt three merry maidens
>   Upon a distant hill,
> One was tall Meggan,
>   And one was dainty May,
> But one was fair Margaret,
>   More fair than I can say,
> Long ago and long ago.

It is artificial, of course, but it really does recapture a note from the very beginning of modern European literature—the songs which, seven hundred years before, the women of France had sung as they worked at their embroidery. The poem of which the lines quoted above are the opening, *Maiden Song*, seem to belong to a golden age of freshness and innocence.

The wide range and consistently high standard attained by Christina Rossetti are more considerable than anyone who has read only those of her poems which have been made over-familiar by the anthologists may imagine. Besides writing romantic and devotional poems, she occasionally displays a certain delicate power of wit, peculiarly feminine, which, nevertheless, women poets have too seldom exercised. Here is her poem *The Queen of Hearts*:

> How comes it, Flora, that whenever we
> Play cards together, you invariably,
>   However the pack parts,
>   Still hold the Queen of Hearts?

I've scanned you with a scrutinizing gaze,
Resolved to fathom these your secret ways;
 But, sift them as I will,
 Your ways are secret still.

I cut and shuffle; shuffle, cut again;
But all my cutting, shuffling, proves in vain;
 Vain hope, vain forethought too;
 That Queen still falls to you.

I dropped her once, prepense; but, ere the deal
Was dealt, your instinct seemed her loss to feel;
 "There should be one card more"
 You said, and searched the floor.

I cheated once; I made a private notch
In Heart-Queen's back, and kept a lynx-eyed watch;
 Yet such another back
 Deceived me in the pack:

The Queen of Clubs assumed by arts unknown,
An imitative dint that seemed my own;
 This notch, not of my doing,
 Misled me to my ruin.

It baffles me to puzzle out the clue,
Which must be skill or craft or luck in you;
 Unless indeed, it be
 Natural affinity.

These lines have a perfection that reminds us of the most delicate art of the eighteenth century.

A brief note may be appended on Richard Watson Dixon, another Anglican poet who was associated with the pre-Raphaelite movement. Dixon was a member of the original "brotherhood"—which included, besides Dixon himself, Morris and Burne-Jones. These three shared in common a vague aspiration to regenerate the world by the cultivation of beauty, but their original ideals were literary and poetical, rather than artistic. It was largely the influence of Rossetti

that turned their interests in the direction of painting;
Burne-Jones himself records, that in his Oxford days, he
knew nothing of that subject. Dixon himself soon found that
he had no talent for painting. He entered, as he had intended,
Holy Orders, and in later life became Canon of Carlisle
Cathedral, and a Church historian of distinction. He was
also a friend of Bridges and Hopkins, and although he found
difficulty in understanding Hopkins's verse, it is probable
that he sympathized more closely with the inner spiritual
struggle which informed it.

Dixon himself has been neglected by readers of poetry, and
ill-served by anthologists. His principal work, *Mano*, a long
narrative poem in *terza rima* on a mediæval subject, is, it
must be admitted, not very readable. Much of his other work
is unadventurously descriptive, or too closely imitative of
the manner of Keats, but the best of his religious verse has
quite remarkable qualities, which remind us of Coleridge or
Blake. His poem, *The Wizard's Funeral*, will serve to illustrate how he endues a romantic theme with a more than
usual consciousness of the presence of Good and Evil:

> For me, for me, two horses wait,
> Two horses stand before my gate:
> Their vast black plumes on high are cast,
> Their black manes swing in the midnight blast,
> Red sparkles from their eyes fly fast.
> But can they drag the hearse behind,
> Whose black plumes mystify the wind?
> What a thing for this heap of bones and hair!
> Despair, despair!
> Yet think of half the world's winged shapes
> Which have come to thee wondering:
> At thee the terrible idiot gapes,
> At thee the running devil japes,
> And angels stoopt to thee and sing
> From the soft midnight that enwraps
> Their limbs so gently, sadly fair;—
> Thou seest the stars shine through their hair.

The blast again, ho, ho, the blast!
I go to a mansion that shall outlast;
And the stoled priest who stops before
Shall turn and welcome me at the door.

Dixon's style is not greatly influenced by that of the pre-Raphaelites—though his poem on Saint Mary Magdalen has something of the same detailed, pictorial quality as has theirs:

Kneeling before the altar step,
    Her white face stretched above her hands;
In one great line her body thin
Rose robed right upwards to her chin;
Her hair rebelled in golden bands,
    And filled her hands.

He is rather a scholarly, visionary mediævalist, such as we have already encountered in the person of Robert Stephen Hawker. His work serves to remind us of the close connection between the pre-Raphaelite aestheticism and visionary and mystical tendencies within the Church which were contemporary with it.

The character of William Morris, the vigorous advocate of Socialism and the practical craftsman, presents a striking contrast to that of Rossetti. His personality was fuller, saner, more "rounded", than that of almost any other of his contemporaries. But his poetry represents only a fragment of that personality, and in some ways the least vital part of it. The withdrawal from the external world is more complete in William Morris, the poet, than in any other of the pre-Raphaelites, and his treatment of mediæval subject-matter is more consistent. It is often said that he had a "mediæval mind"; but he lacked the spiritual sense of the mediæval man, and with it, that very earthy realism which is its complement. It is significant that there is no humour in Morris—least of all the gross, animal comedy of the *Fabliaux*; no Wife of Bath, no Miller of Trumpington, no *buttocks*; not even the comic Skelton, that postures and capers through the poetry of the fifteenth century, as the curtain falls upon the mediæval scene. Morris's world is illuminated by an unreal light. He does not, indeed, sentimentalize the Middle Ages —he knew his mediæval literature too well for that; there is the real passion and brutality of primitive times in the *Haystack in the Floods*. The delineation of the knights and squires of his stories is masculine—perhaps too masculine. Was there not, for all the bloody times in which they lived, a streak of adolescent femininity in the members of a class who delighted to hear stories and songs of Courtly Love, even if this strange code was always more a matter of theory than of practice? It is not this which gives to Troilus or to Arcite —they were little more than boys, after all—their pathos? And we remember too Richard II—and Edward II.

Morris's love for Chaucer was genuine, and he often set out deliberately to imitate his style. But in truth he was less at home in Chaucer's complex and sophisticated world, than in that of the Icelandic Sagas and the oldest poetry of the North—a world untouched by the new flowering of intellectualism which arose in twelfth-century Paris, or by the strange imaginative movement that spread from Provence at about the same time. The Iceland of the Sagas preserved an older and simpler social structure than the rest of Europe; it received its Christianity late, and much of the tradition, at least, of pre-Christian times lingered on.

The response of these men to life was, like that of Morris himself, simple, direct, temperate. Getting a living on the island was too strenuous a business to allow time for speculation, metaphysical or emotional; the Icelanders were not tormented by the problems which beset the men of the later Middle Ages throughout the rest of Europe. Even so apparently cheerful and unintrospective a mind as Chaucer's is obsessed by the philosophical problem of Free Will, and how it may be reconciled with God's foreknowledge. For the men of the Sagas, Fate is important; but it is something that can only be met with steadfast courage—like that half-pagan concept of *Wyrd* of the Anglo-Saxons.

Morris's translations and adaptations from the Sagas are much more vigorous than his earlier work; the languid style of the *Early Romances* gives place to the galloping metre of *Sigurd the Volsung*. But we miss the matter-of-factness, the plainness, the gruff and sometimes grim humour of the Saga-men. Above all, Morris's deliberate quaintness in his choice of language blurs the outlines of his originals.

In his treatment of stories from antique sources, Morris hardly either gives them a new significance for his own age, or penetrates to their living core. Let us remember that the legends of the mediæval story-tellers, like the myths of the Ancients, however remote from reality they may seem to us, had, as their background, the manners and social life of the times that produced them. In the Romances of chivalry the heroes often seem to us to be placed in fantastic situations, but these situations, and the problems of conduct arising out of them, reflected those which might occur in real life. To take a rather trite example: a princess in real life might not require rescuing from a dragon or giant, but an heiress or a widow might, under circumstances in all respects parallel, have need of a champion against a powerful neighbour who ravaged her lands, or who sought to coerce her into marriage in order to force her to join her fiefs to his. Similarly, when a mediæval poet speaks of fighting, or armour, or fortification, he does not allow his eye to stray from what he is describing. He has too much professional interest in these matters. A modern poet treating an archaic subject, has either to give such things and the whole scene of his story a fresh significance for his readers, or by an effort of the imagination, pierce through to what was vital for the men of former times. Neither of these was Morris's mind strenuous enough to affect. His treatment of the old stories is fundamentally decorative; he tells them as he wove tapestry, or designed wallpaper. They are spun out at too great a length, and their beauty is merely a surface beauty of imagery with nothing lying beneath to satisfy the intellect and emotions. Archaicisms and affectations of language apart, he has probably one of the purest poetical styles, in its natural easy flow, of the century—in striking contrast to the vulgarity and heaviness of Rossetti; but it is too diffuse to leave any definite impression on the mind. It is the same with his characters; only the queen in the early *Defence of Guenevere* seems to have a vitality of her own. At moments in this poem does Morris achieve that concentrated passion, an image which continually haunts the memory.

It is significant that nearly all the members of the original Oxford "Brotherhood", among which the germ from which the whole pre-Raphaelite movement sprung was nursed, were young men intending to enter Holy Orders, and of the High Church party. Morris was no exception to this, but he seems to have changed his intention and wandered into the by-paths of agnosticism without any of the spiritual torments which usually accompanied loss of religious convictions among the Victorians. It would be true to say, perhaps, that his Christianity slipped from him, and was never missed. Whereas Rossetti is a visionary, without any clear basis of faith that might give reality to his visions, Morris has been described as a natural pagan. His was a primitive mind, not troubled by the complexities suggested by the existence of suffering and evil. He saw these things, indeed, embodied in the industrialism that lay about him, but he did not apprehend them imaginatively, as Blake apprehended the "dark, satanic mills", or even as Tennyson had expressed them in *Maud*. Following Ruskin, he simply envisaged the machine as banished from the ideal society of the future. His natural belief was on the capacity of men spontaneously to develop and to attain happiness, if only those things which check that development can be removed. Hence he advocated a form of Socialism, in its essential ideals nearer to Anarchism. The world he represents in his poetry is really less mediæval than pagan, and embodies his vision of a simple, spontaneous life.

The story-telling pilgrims of Chaucer are journeying to find the shrine of saint and martyr. The shrine is situated in a definite place in England, and the martyr suffered at a definite time. The narrators of Morris's longest poem sail away from a vague mediæval world, to seek an Earthly Paradise. They do not find it, but discover instead a fragment of pagan antiquity, timelessly surviving in the western ocean. The ideal society which Morris envisaged in *News from Nowhere* is also an earthly paradise—a mediæval dream-world, very unlike the actual Middle Ages. The only deeper emotion which disturbs the vision of Morris's poetry is the fear of death, a subdued undertone which sounds through much of his verse like the sound of the sea which echoes beyond the garden of bare apple-trees in the nymph's song to Hylas.

Swinburne is, rightly, classed with the pre-Raphaelite poets. He was a close friend of Morris and Rossetti, with whom he first came into contact in his Oxford days. His early poetry especially—notably *A Ballad of Life* and *The Mask of Queen Bathsabe*—has much the same languorous, decorative quality as theirs, the same attitude to mediæval subject-matter, and many of the same tricks of diction. But unlike them, he was never a visual poet. He was incapable of their minute concentration or particular natural images, and uses words in an almost purely aural manner. Moreover his poetry seems to stand in a wider context than theirs. At first sight it looks like a continuation of the Romantic tradition of Shelley and Byron, which brought a lyrical rhetoric and devotion to liberty, as well as purely private experience, within its scope. Swinburne's verse exhibits the appearance of a development from a preoccupation with merely erotic themes, in *Poems and Ballads*, to the public poetry of *Songs before Sunrise*. But this is largely an illusion. Throughout his writings, Swinburne remains virtually cut off from any save literary and verbal experience. His political poems, read to-day, betray, by their vague rhetoric, their unreality. He is an almost purely aesthetic poet.

None of the more important Victorian poets is more difficult to read, with any pleasure, to-day, than Swinburne. His contemporaries, and the generation which followed, even though they objected to the content of his poetry, or to its lack of definite meaning, were unanimous in according the very highest praise to the music of his verse. But the modern ear is attuned to more subtle rhythms. We have been taught by Hopkins and by the poets of our own day to expect in the music of poetry, however intricate, an underlying basis of natural speech-rhythms. We have also rediscovered the exquisite variety produced by the skilful arrangement of pause and syllable within the narrow framework of Pope's couplet— which the nineteenth century voted monotonous—and in Donne, not the harshness which had come to be traditionally associated with his name by critics, but a fine, natural music. For us it is precisely in the matter of musical delight that Swinburne fails to satisfy. His rhythms are mechanical, his heavily stressed anapæstic and dactylic metres vulgar, his use of pause often lacking in subtlety; though a certain facility in the melodic arrangement of vowel sounds must be granted him—it comes out best in his slower-moving pieces, such as *A Leave-Taking*:

> Let us go hence, go hence; she will not see.
> Sing all once more together; surely she,
> She too, remembering days and words that were,
> Will turn a little towards us, sighing; but we,
> We are hence, we are gone, as though we had not been there,
> Nay, and though all men seeing had pity on me,
>   She would not see.

In order to appreciate Swinburne's style, it is best to read his poems in chronological order, as they came before the Victorian public, and with the poetic standards against which his verse instituted a reaction in mind the while. Here is Tennyson's "classical" style at its best—the much and deservedly praised *Ulysses*:

> I cannot rest from travel; I will drink
> Life to the lees; all times I have enjoyed
> Greatly, have suffer'd greatly, both with those
> That lov'd me and alone; on shore, and when
> Thro' scudding drifts the rainy Hyades
> Vext the dim sea; I am become a name;
> For always roaming with a hungry heart . . .

But here are the opening lines of *Atalanta in Calydon*:

> Maiden and mistress of the months and stars
> Now folded in the flowerless fields of heaven,
> Goddess whom all gods love with threefold heart,
> Being treble in thy divided Deity,
> A light for dead men and dark hours, a foot
> Swift on the hills as morning, and a hand
> To all things fierce and fleet that roar and rage
> Mortal, with gentler shafts than snow or sleep;
> Hear now and help . . .

There is a swiftness and grace of movement, a clear melodic quality, about these lines, that must have seemed a fresh wind after the dusty academicism of much of Arnold and Tennyson's Hellenizing, the fusty antiquarianism of Browning—and, above all, the monstrous unpruned growths of Mrs. Browning and the now forgotten "Spasmodic" school. We read on, with this in mind, till we reach the famous choruses; and they—even the hackneyed "When the hounds of Spring . . . "—seem to leap from the page with a new lyrical vitality. We begin to wonder whether we had not too harshly condemned Swinburne. This hesitation, alas, does not survive a methodical critical scrutiny of the poetry. We soon detect the unnecessary diffuseness, the meaninglessness of phrase after phrase, the vagueness of the sensuous imagery, the cheap tricks of pointless antithesis, the tasteless affectation of pseudo-biblical diction. These choric

rhythms too—they are not really *alive*: they repeat themselves indefinitely—there is no sense of climax, musically led
up to and achieved. The long breathless sentences sprout
subsidiary clauses and phrases, without providing logical
cadence for the mind, or—read them aloud—pause for the
voice. Moreover, in the course of the rapid flowering and
long running to seed of Swinburne's genius, these initial faults
become more marked. There are traces of genuinely imaginative, though immature passion in *Atalanta*; but it gives place
first to the crude sensationalism of the *Poems and Ballads* and
then to the vague rhetoric of *Songs before Sunrise*. But his
later work—for he continued to write industriously right up
to the time of his death—consists largely of mere agglomera-
tions of words, moving with a kind of spurious life of their
own—it can hardly be called poetry at all.

Swinburne's psychological abnormality is quite clearly seen
throughout his work, but especially in the first series of
Poems and Ballads. He was an epileptic and a sado-masochist.
It is also probable that he was sexually impotent. Such a
sensibility will only respond to the crudest physical stimuli;
the astonishing effect of his poetry upon an emotionally
inhibited age is significant. He is continually striving in vain
to render sensuous experience in imaginative terms; but the
objects of sense are always slipping from him, and his imagery
becomes vague and generalized. Hence Swinburne, setting
forth a creed of pagan enjoyment and freedom from restraint,
is himself a poet of frustration and impotence.

It is impossible to gloss over the fact that sadism, often of
a crude type, forms the dominant inspiration of most of
Swinburne's poetry, at any rate in his best period, and expresses itself, in a sublimated form, as Mario Praz has pointed
out in his *The Romantic Agony*, in the political idealism of
Songs before Sunrise. This aspect of his genius is pathological,
but nevertheless one cannot separate his poetry from the
diseased nature of his sensibility, if we are to consider the
former seriously. The exploitation of "sin" and perversion

which marks the first series of *Poems and Ballads* is too systematic to be dismissed, as most English critics have been content to do, as the result of a mere youthful desire to shock, Swinburne had become acquainted with the works of the Marquis de Sade in the library of his friend Lord Houghton, and their influence on him was profound, and moreover lasting. From this source he took over this conception of God as a hostile, deliberately cruel power, which permeates *Atalanta*; among the *Poems and Ballads*, *Anactoria* is full of echoes of de Sade's doctrine:

> . . . but were I made as he
> Who hath made all things to break them one by one,
> If my feet trod upon the stars and sun
> And souls of men as his have always trod,
> God knows I might be crueller than God.
> For who shall change with prayers of thanksgivings
> The mystery of the cruelty of things?
> Or say what God above all gods and years,
> With offering and blood-sacrifice of tears,
> With lamentations from strange lands, from graves
> Where the snake pastures, from starved mouths of slaves,
> From prison, and from plunging prows of ships
> Through flamelike foam of the sea's closing lips—
> With thwartings of strange signs, and wind-blown hair
> Of comets, desolating the dim air,
> When darkness is made fast with seals and bars,
> And fierce reluctance of disastrous stars,
> Eclipse, and sound of shaken hills, and wings
> Darkening, and blind inexpiable things—
> With sorrow of labouring moons, and altering light
> And travail of the planets of the night,
> And weeping of the weary Pleiads seven,
> Feeds the mute melancholy lust of heaven?

The idea of the essentially sadistic nature of love dominates not only such poems as *Dolores*, *Faustine*, etc., but also the whole of the drama of *Chastelard*. In the first *Poems and*

Ballads indeed, Swinburne introduces us into a world of sterile perversity, which, nevertheless, has a kind of lifeless reality of its own. Perhaps the best of the series is *Hermaphroditus*, which consists in reality of a group of sonnets, to which form Swinburne has given back the essential lyrical quality which had been lost for it. Something more than mere verbalism is realized in this poem. The hermaphrodite, ambiguous and virginal, because unable to respond to the desire of either sex, yet apt to satisfy both, really does represent a *moment* in the history of European Romanticism, and links Swinburne to such Continental decadents as Lautréamont.

> Love stands upon thy left hand and thy right,
>   Yet by no sunset and by no moonrise
>   Shall make thee man and ease a woman's sighs,
> Or make thee woman for a man's delight.
> To what strange end hath some strange god made fair
>   The double blossom of two different flowers?
> Hid love in all the folds of all thy hair,
>   Fed thee on summers, watered thee with showers
> Given all the gold that all the seasons wear
>   To thee that art a thing of barren hours?

If the *Hermaphroditus* sonnets reveal the core of Swinburne's poetry—the prenatal, undifferentiated, embryonic form to which his maladjustment leads him to desire a return—*The Triumph of Time*, from another point of view, provides the key to his peculiar experience. It has often been singled out as showing more genuine personal feeling than his other poems. It celebrates, as is well known, his feelings when rejected by Jane Simon, to whom he had proposed marriage. It is too long, and there is a good deal too much self-pity in it. But here, at least, the Swinburnian deadness and monotony of rhythm—that wave-like, rocking rhythm—is appropriate. This unhappy love affair represented for Swinburne his defeat. Henceforward for him there was no possiblity of a normal adjustment to life, and he turns from the girl who has failed him and left him unprotected against the sadistic passions within him, to the sea, which is at once a mother and womb symbol, and the image of the cold, grey, harsh, and salty sterility which was to be henceforward his.

> I will go back to the great sweet mother,
>   Mother and lover of men, the sea,
> I will go down to her, I and none other,
>   Close with her, kiss her, and mix her with me;
> Cling to her, strive with her, hold her fast:
> O fair white mother, in days long past
> Born without sister, born without brother,
>   Set free my soul as thy soul is free.

To appreciate Swinburne to-day we must not only bear his abnormal nature in mind, but also read him less in relation to his English forerunners, Shelley and the pre-Raphaelites, and as an outlier of the Continental Romantic-Decadent Movement. We remember his mother, Lady Swinburne, and her enthusiasm for French and Italian poetry, and Swinburne's own interest in European politics. (He is really our first poet since Byron who showed himself genuinely aware of Europe.) Above all we must bear in mind the influence on him not only of Gautier and Baudelaire but also of Hugo (for whom Yeats also, in spite of his symbolist doctrines, retained a lifelong admiration, and whose vatic conception of the poet's function the Irish poet largely adopted for himself).

It is, however, especially when we compare him with Baudelaire that the inadequacy of Swinburne as a poet becomes apparent. Swinburne celebrated Baudelaire in *Ave atque Vale* as a "brother", but the difference between them is in reality profound. The psychology of both gives ample evidence of a sado-masochistic tendency, and both show direct acquaintance with the ideas of the Marquis de Sade. The deep-rooted connection between love and the infliction,

12

or receiving of pain which formed the basis of de Sade's crude speculations, is a fact of which the Christian religion had preserved the intuition. The psychology of Baudelaire and Swinburne was abnormal, but their abnormality only brought into prominence what is a normal condition of human nature. But whereas Baudelaire's genius leads him to a profound poetical investigation of the nature of evil, Swinburne's abnormality merely drives him into a sterile verbalism and sensationalism.

Chapter 6

BEYOND AESTHETICISM

THE poetry of Swinburne represents a dead end. Though the closing decades of the nineteenth century saw the triumph of the doctrine of art for art's sake, a tendency is discernible in the work of the most considerable of those poets whose careers began in the 'eighties and 'nineties, and ended in the earlier part of the twentieth century, to widen the scope of poetry once more. But the reaction is less towards the rhetoric and realism which the generation of Tennyson had sometimes favoured, than an attempt, in some measure, to use the symbols and images of aesthetic experience itself as a basis from which to discover a coherent imaginative picture of the universe.

In these writers we see the beginning of the poetry of our own age; for it is its character of metaphysical integrity, I believe, which is really typical of modern poetry at its best. But it is important to emphasize that this modern poetry has its roots in the Aesthetic Movement—either pre-Raphaelite or Symbolist—and in the Romantic tradition, against which it has been so often in revolt. The modern poet who deliberately rejects the Romantic tradition, rejects an experience through which the European consciousness has passed, and which has affected it profoundly. If we are aiming at a classical ideal, it will be necessary for us to accept what is valid in Romanticism as part of the means whereby that ideal may be approached. I have tried to show that Aestheticism —which has been so often whole-heartedly condemned in our day by critics who (rightly perhaps) have stressed the social nature of poetry—represents a necessary strategic withdrawal into the inner strongholds of the imagination in the face of an uncompromising materialism. The experience

of the Aesthete, also, must be accepted if we are to understand aright the true nature and development of our living
poetic tradition.

George Meredith, who though he was associated with the
original pre-Raphaelite circle, survived into the present century, might be taken, to some extent, as representing this
transition from Aestheticism to an imaginative Realism. But
he remains, on the whole, more Victorian than modern in his
outlook and technique. His real affinities are with Browning;
he has the same uncertain ear and imperfect sense of form, the
same love for melodrama and the grotesque and, at his best, a
similar sensibility for concrete imagery. But his is an inferior
and coarser imagination than Browning's—fundamentally
less poetic. His "philosophy" is even less vitally related to the
form of his poetry, his thought less imaginatively felt, than
is the case with Browning; and it is a shallow enough
philosophy at that. In some respects Meredith may be regarded as one who carried on the "Realistic" tradition in
English poetry from Browning to the moderns, and there is
more concentration—less of that fatal Victorian fustiness and
diffuseness—about his way of writing than in that of the
earlier poet. But on the whole there is little in Meredith that
had not been done rather better by Browning. A certain
freshness in his response to natural life occasionally recom-
mends itself to our attention; his poem *Young Reynard* has a
little of the quality of Hopkins:

> Gracefullest leaper, the dappled fox-cub
> Curves over brambles with berries and buds,
> Light as a bubble that flies from the tub
> Whisked by the laundry wife out of her suds,
> Wavy he comes, woody, all at his ease,
> Elegant, fashioned to foot with the deuce;
> Nature's own prince of the dance: then he sees
> Me, and retires as if making excuse.

Modern Love remains, perhaps, his most notable achievement. Some have seen the Meredith of this sequence of poems
as a successor of Byron. They form a good example of a genre
rather characteristic of the later nineteenth century—the
verse-novel. In a period when the novel had usurped the
central place in imaginative literature which had once been
held by epic and Romantic narrative poetry, we find a
number of poets making tentative raids into the invader's
territory. Browning's *Ring and the Book* came nearest, perhaps, to success. But there were also *The Angel in the House*,
Maud, Mrs. Browning's *Aurora Leigh*, the two realistic
narrative poems of Clough already referred to, and several
others. But in all of these we cannot help feeling that the
form sits uneasily upon the matter. The poets are in doubt,
also, what form to choose in order to produce in verse something equivalent to the novel. Mrs. Browning, the least
original poet, chooses the most straightforward way—versification of a direct novelistic plot. Browning evolved a form
more truly his own, out of the dramatic monologue. Patmore
and Tennyson remain essentially lyrical, while Clough's
poems descend, via Longfellow's *Evangeline*, from Goethe's
Hermann and Dorothea. Another and broader model might
have been provided by Byron's *Don Juan*, derived as it is
from the fantastical realistic tradition of the Italian comic
epic of Pulci and others. But the Victorian fought a little shy
of this side of Byron's genius. Byronic influence is, however,
discernible in *Modern Love*, as it is in another verse-novel
which we shall examine in more detail presently—Blunt's
Esther. Both these poems, however, in regard to their form,
derive not from an epic model, but from the sonnet sequence.
This was a very natural and beautiful piece of evolution;
there is already a good deal of the suggestion of a novelist's
technique in the sonnet sequence, even as early as Sidney's
Astrophel and Stella.

Some of Meredith's verse, notably the *Hymn to Colour*,
does represent an attempt to build a metaphysical poetry

upon purely aesthetic experience. Such a course had to be followed, if aesthetic poetry was to be redeemed from mere decorativeness, though Meredith did not possess a sufficiently sensitive imagination to accomplish it. Platonism, with its idea of absolute beauty, was a philosophic tradition whereby such an aesthetic metaphysic might be constructed. More esoteric doctrines of neo-Platonic affinities, derived ultimately from German Idealism, furnished an intellectual basis for the Symbolist theory of poetry in France. In England, however, there was a classical example of more or less Christianized Platonism transmuted into poetry in the work of Spenser, which occupied a central place in the literary tradition. Romantic criticism, from Hazlitt downwards had tended to relegate Spenser to the position of a merely decorative and fantastic poet; but in fact the *Four Hymnes* and many passages in the *Faerie Queene* reveal him as a genuine, if not a great, philosophical poet. His genius can hardly be reckoned akin to Lucretius'—yet with how little incongruity does the masterly translation of the Roman poet's invocation to Venus take its place in the fourth book of the *Faerie Queene*. Something of Spenser's intellectual quality, as well as of his sensuous imagery, had passed to Keats—the Keats of the Odes; but it was altered by the later poet's very different personality. Now that poetry had been forced to fall back upon its aesthetic strongholds, could not that quality be revived?

Robert Bridges's poetry began to appear in the late 'seventies. From first to last he was a representative of the tradition of English verse which passed from Spenser to Milton and Keats, and he was singularly unsusceptible to alien influences. He aimed at a "pure" and "classical" style, looking back to the Elizabethans and the Greeks, but appears to have been little influenced by the Tennysonian richness, or the characteristic mannerisms of the pre-Raphaelites. In later life he seems to have shown no love for the seventeenth-century "Metaphysicals" which were then becoming fashionable. He was, in most other respects, a very typical Victorian in his tastes, but he appears never to have conquered an aversion to Browning's roughness and obscurity. Yet, though he stands apart from the main current of the Aesthetic Movement, his early work was entirely decorative and melodious in character. Yeats, in 1898, in his essay *The Autumn of the Body*, remarking and welcoming a revolution in English poetry which, according to him, began with Rossetti and was parallel to that effected by the Symbolists in France, singles out for praise Bridges, who "elaborated a rhythm too delicate for any but an almost bodiless emotion, and repeated over and over the most ancient notes of poetry, and none but these". Yet when, in 1929, at the end of his long life, Bridges produced *The Testament of Beauty*, a poem philosophical and didactic in content, he had not departed from the path on which he had entered in his earlier work. It was natural that so thoughtful and scholarly a mind, having reached maturity, should seek to elaborate into a system the evidence of reality presented to it by the aesthetic experiences which had gone to the making of his first poems. *The Testament* is essentially a product of the Aesthetic Movement, since it is from the fact of man's response to Beauty that the whole argument is developed. In reading the philosophical poetry of Browning and Meredith we feel that there is no essential unity of form and content, no organic interrelation of the musical pattern of the verse, the sensuous character of the images, and the elaborated thought. The same cannot wholly be said of *The Testament of Beauty*. Here the thought reacts upon the form throughout, so that a new and delicate metrical pattern is evolved, whose music is an essential expression of the evolution of the poet's argument. The abstract terms employed in the poem are used precisely, and false rhetoric is everywhere absent. Throughout it is through images that the poet feels his thought. Yet in spite of this, and the high praise lavished upon it by critics at its first appearance, the poem cannot be accounted great philosophical poetry.

That is not primarily because its arguments may be refuted.

I believe purely philosophical poetry to be a perfectly possible and legitimate species of composition (though many have denied this), provided its argument is transmuted through the medium of the poet's imagination. A true philosophic poem is born of an acute intellectual experience. The poet is conscious of a vision of the universe whereby the problems and doubts which had beset him seem to be resolved; and this vision has come to him by way of purely intellectual speculations and arguments. As a poet, then, he seeks to transmit to his audience the reasoned clarity of this vision. Lucretius' *De Rerum Natura* arises from such an experience. The poet is not the mere versifier of philosophical arguments, but seeks, by presenting the evident truth of those arguments as he sees them, to redeem his hearers from superstition and fear. Hence, in philosophical poetry, it is not ultimately necessary that the arguments employed should be valid, but that they should present the appearance of validity to the imagination. The poet himself must, in fact, believe in them; his readers must be able to suspend their unbelief. For the arguments play exactly the same part in the work of a philosophical poet, as mythology does in that of a poet who records his vision through the epic or dramatic medium.

Yet though *The Testament of Beauty* is genuinely the expression of an imaginative intellectual experience, the vision itself is not, I think, of sufficient intensity or universal application. The development of Bridges—from the purely decorative preoccupations of his earlier work towards a philosophical poetry, whose arguments are primarily based upon aesthetic experience—is typical of the aesthetic poets of his generation and that which immediately followed it. These were the men who continued to develop and lived through the great social and intellectual changes precipitated by the 1914–18 war, into the more strenuous atmosphere of the new Europe.

The development of Yeats offers a parallel, and that of Rilke an even closer one, though these poets were in the

European Symbolist movement, whose influence left Bridges untouched. But to mention Bridges alongside these two great poets, is at once to reveal the smallness of his stature, compared with theirs. Bridges's poetical horizon is too narrow; *The Testament of Beauty* is so patently the product of a scholarly, sheltered, middle-class English mind. He is, in fact, the perfect academic poet; and one suspects that it is only in academic, or near-academic circles, that he still enjoys any fame, or indeed finds any readers to-day. Among such circles he had, at the end of his life, many friends and not a little influence. I have an idea that his name is kept before the public by means of a sort of ghost-reputation, supported still among those same circles. If one were to read carefully all the lectures and theses on the theory of poetry which from time to time emanate from our universities, and from the information thus absorbed were to construct a sort of artificial Frankenstein monster of a great poet according to specification, that poet would be as like Bridges as makes no difference. But in life every truly great poet contains within himself a spark of the unaccountable and unexpected, which it is beyond the power of critical theorizing to define. It is this spark which makes each great poet absolutely unique, so that, by his advent, the very nature of poetry itself is altered. And it was this spark, this unknown quantity, which was totally lacking in Bridges.

When we come to examine *The Testament of Beauty* we find that its formal originality, though real, is timid; and it is the expression of its content. There is no consciousness in the poem of the abysses of passion and of evil which surround the naked spirit of man in the universe. Bridges, sheltered among his books in comfortable security, had not glimpsed these things. And his conception of Beauty, from which the whole poem takes its rise, is equally limited. For him, Beauty is a quiet enjoyment, not a passion. This is not classical temperance; *that* in the Greeks arose from a discipline imposed upon senses vivid and tumultuous.

I had not dwelt so long upon Bridges's poem if it did not typify so clearly what had happened to the purely English, central and, as it were, official literary tradition in his generation. The prosperity which had come to our middle classes enabled them, to a great extent, to ignore the social and economic forces which were changing the face of Europe, and the need for new patterns in thought and art. Industrial capitalism, indeed, had reached its crisis; but in England, in the last years of the nineteenth century and the beginning of the twentieth, there was no imminent threat of civil war or revolution. An era of Imperialist expansion prompted a mood of optimism in those who enjoyed its fruits. The minor aesthetic poets of the 'nineties whose more romantic imagination this mood could not satisfy, became to some extent outcasts, though they were not driven into any active revolt against society. The popular poetry of the day has soon to be exemplified by the verse of Kipling, Sir Henry Newbolt, and Sir William Watson. These three poets (to whom it would be invidious to add the name of Alfred Austin) represent the voice of late Victorian and Edwardian imperialism. It is a crude, brassy, and often frankly vulgar voice. Watson deserves to be remembered for his invectives against the Turk, in which real indignation is called forth by a worthy cause. But I doubt if one line of genuine poetry is discoverable in the work of this pompous and frigid rhetorician, the ghost of whose once considerable poetic reputation still lingers on in some quarters. It is tempting to dismiss Newbolt as no more than a minor Kipling. This is not the whole truth; his patriotic verse, though doubtless he never knew it, is a sham. In reality, though, he had a genuine vein of poetry, which he worked too seldom, unless in his latter years, when he came under the personal influence of Bridges: an inborn, somewhat nostalgic feeling for the English countryside, the tradition of English life, and a sensitive apprehension of death—as such poems as *From Generation to Generation* show.

Kipling himself is not so easily to be written off. He is a

genuine poet, as well as an exceedingly competent craftsman, with a wide range and a consistent vision. His patriotism is not a gentlemanly fantasy. His realism is in fact intense and brutal, and he understood the psychology of the professional soldier. His earlier poems were written to speak for that neglected class of men by whose efforts and out of whose suffering the Empire in which he believed had been built up. In his later work he largely created for his generation a myth of Empire. It is easy to underrate Kipling, simply because one holds that Empire to have been, in fact, no more than a vast fabric of oppression and exploitation. It may have been; so in fact was the Roman Empire—yet that inspired the great and wonderful poetic vision of Virgil, which haunts Europe still.

Nevertheless, it is obvious that Kipling was no Virgil. There is a radical insensitiveness about his writing, a sort of Puritan brutality which is repulsive, and the very reverse of the noble and sensitive humanism of the Roman poet. It is no accident that one of the most memorable of Kipling's poems should be *McAndrew's Hymn*. McAndrew (a Scotch Calvinist) adores the impersonal, inhuman power of his machine. It is prophetic of our time, and of much that is most sinister in it. Far more than his imperialism it suggests that Kipling was a forerunner of totalitarianism. In this glorification of the machine, the symbol of inhuman strength and power, there is none of the disordered sensibility which was later to make the work of the so-called Futurists— Marinetti or Mayakowsky—or Hart Crane's desperate striving to bring about the consummation of the marriage of Faustus and Helen. Kipling accepts quite simply and naturally an image of the machine which is the death of poetry. Similarly we find in him, and his followers, that mechanical, lifeless quality of rhythm, which, beginning from Swinburne, seemed fast to be becoming the only voice by which the age could express itself.

Bridges stands apart from these poets, and the amateurish

Georgian pastoralists who succeeded them, and of whom he himself was largely the public godfather, by virtue of a certain scholarly integrity and craftsmanship. His Platonism and his real love and knowledge of the classics and that tradition of English literature of which he was himself a representative, prevented his imagination from losing its sensitive quality. In a way, he deserved the honoured position that he at last won among the poets of his day. But read against its historical European background, his poetry is seen at once to be thin and unreal. In truth the polite English *littérateurs* of whom he was an example might have been wholly unaware of any contemporary European writing for all the influence it had upon their work. Yeats, in an Ireland torn by civil war, is much more a poet of European significance. And it was left to two Americans with an international European culture —Ezra Pound and T. S. Eliot—finally to break down the complacency of the English poetic tradition. By this time there was left no native poet, even among those in revolt, of sufficient stature to do so without their lead.

C. M. Doughty, in his systematic attempt to form, as Spenser and Milton had formed, a synthetic dialect for heroic poetry, evinces an attitude to his art in some ways similar to Bridges, though he is more profoundly akin, in his revolutionary approach to language, to Bridges's friend, Hopkins. For him the right line of English poetry practically ended with his acknowledged master, Spenser. His conception of the nature of the historical development of poetry is summed up in the prose note which he places after the conclusion of *The Dawn in Britain*. He begins by acknowledging Homer, as "father of European, (as distinguished from the yet earlier Asiatic and Egyptian) poetic art", and then pays tribute to Chaucer and Spenser as the fathers of the same art in "this North-lying island soil". After this, "the kindled stream of song has since flowed down in two channels. The one following the fruitful Homeric tradition (which revived, from long living death, in the classical *Renaissance*); the

other a self-sprung bardism; now, it is said, like Abana and
Pharpar, nearly run out to the dregs, and unwholesome pools
in the desert." He sought to recover this pristine European
tradition which began from Homer and had been disrupted
by the self-sprung bardism of the Romantics. In his primi-
tivist ideal of poetry he is akin to the pre-Raphaelites, particularly to Morris, but his verse is not, like theirs, decorative.
He was able to penetrate far more deeply than they into
the consciousness of the life of primitive times. In his most
important work, *The Dawn in Britain,* he creates a world of
his own, which is at the same time archaic and eternal.
Though none of his poetry was published till the early years
of this century, he was planning it in the sixties of the last.
His Arabian travels, of which was born his prose work *Arabia
Deserta,* were, in a sense, part of this long preparation. By
contact with older cultures, and men whose response to life
was simpler and fresher than those of cultivated Europeans,
he sought to rediscover that primitive poetic feeling which
we find in the world's great early epics.

In the stress and hurry of modern life there is perhaps every
excuse for a certain hesitation before attempting to read an
epic in twenty-four books; nevertheless, it is the only full-
length epic poem in English which might not be lessened in
comparison with Milton's masterpiece; but it is so different
and individual in style and subject—owing nothing to the
manner of the earlier poet but what both have inherited from
Homer—that such a comparison is not called for. In Milton
the lyrical and subjective side of his nature is not wholly
absorbed in his epic theme. It is possible to lift passages of
Paradise Lost from their context and treat them as separate
lyrics.[1] Doughty's epic style is firmer and cannot be so
treated. The words are made to bear the greatest weight of
meaning, and to obey "the logic of passion" as in a synthetic
language, but the syntax is not, as in Milton, involved; the

[1] As Sir Arthur Quiller-Couch has actually seen fit to do in the *Oxford Book
of English Verse.* It is surely doing Milton scant courtesy.

sentences are even abrupt, and the style extraordinarily lucid. The subjective character of Milton's mind is seen also in the way he handles his material; the struggle is often an internal one in the mind of Adam or Satan, and the proportion of mythological debate and of supernatural machinery to human action is greater than in any of his models. The essentially non-primitive and complex nature of Milton's mind sometimes makes his use of Homeric machinery appear forced. It is this, I think, which has made many modern critics instinctively distrust his epic, and condemn his machinery (wrongly) as conventional. In Doughty's poem, the product of a more primitive and serener mind, this difficulty is not felt. It is a story of human action, like the great epics of the world, involving large masses of men in historical movement.

The proper subject of epic poetry is both myth and history. It is the highest and most difficult species of poetry, precisely because it transcends the realm of mere individual invention and fancy, and tells a story which is, in part at least, accepted as *fact* by the reader. But it is not merely historic fact, but racial or religious myth, with a communal, and not only personal significance.

The poets of "primitive" or Homeric epic find this subject-matter in the legends held in common by the race. As civilization becomes more complex, the subject of epic poetry changes, and fact becomes increasingly more difficult to transmute into myth. The history of epic poetry from Virgil to Milton is an epitome of the history of Western European civilization. First we have the myth of the birth of Imperial Rome, then the mediæval Pilgrimage of the Soul, ascending through three worlds of being; then the struggle of Christendom with the Mohammedan East—expanding Christendom in the age of Vasco da Gama planting its triumphs in the Indies, or the romantic dream of the Counter-Reformation, the Holy City delivered. In these terms Camoëns and Tasso continue, on another level, the story of the struggle of East and West, already foreshadowed by Virgil when he figured, in the meeting of Dido and Aeneas, the tragic conflict of Rome and Carthage, or of Octavian and Cleopatra. Finally, there is the Protestant epic of the Fall of Man, in which a biblical myth is made the mould which contains once again the mediæval theme of the struggle of Good and Evil, for Man's soul.

In the English poetry of the period we are surveying, there are only two attempts at epic on the grand scale which need to be seriously considered. Of Hardy's *The Dynasts*, an epic drama rather than a regular epic on the classic model, I have spoken in an earlier chapter, and have suggested that it fails to attain a dignity of style to match the greatness of its conception. In choosing the Napoleonic Wars as his subject, however, Hardy did succeed in selecting the only episode in modern history which could be conceived of as possessing that universal quality of myth, which, I have suggested, is necessary for the conception of epic. It will be obvious, nevertheless, that in dealing with events which have been chronicled with such detail by historians, the poet is hampered. He cannot generalize his materials, reducing them to the simpler, archetypal patterns which epic poetry demands, without forfeiting that belief in the objective truth of what he records, which the epic poet demands of his audience. Hence *The Dynasts* is not pure epic, but in part a chronicle play or historical tragedy. Moreover, Hardy's imagination was limited by his intellectual view of the nature of reality. This necessitates his reducing the traditional epic mythological machinery (necessary to give the sense of a wider, universal context to the poem) to a series of abstract personifications—his Pities, Years, Spirit Ironic, Spirit Sinister, etc.—which are essentially bloodless, and command no real imaginative belief.

Doughty, however, possessed a wider and more matured scholarship than Hardy, and a quality of imagination which enabled him to re-create a primitive, mythopoeic world, in which epic values and machinery do not appear incongruous. The peculiar archaic, yet terse and economical language, which he fashioned for himself, has itself a primitive quality and an essential dignity, fitted to its material. Moreover, Doughty's subject is drawn from a remote and legendary period, outside or on the fringes of history—Britain before and during the Roman conquest, Palestine at the time of the birth of Christianity. For his sources, he goes to the historical authorities—Caesar, Tacitus, Josephus, etc. For his account of early Britain and its kings—with which the greater part of his story deals—he takes hints from modern archaeology, and (but very freely, and in part only) from the fictitious chronicle of Geoffrey of Monmouth, and other mediæval traditions which deal with the first introduction of Christianity into this island. But great lacunae remain, and in these Doughty is at liberty to give his poetic imagination free play, and to reconstruct a pagan, Celtic mythology, on the analogy of that of the Homeric poems.

The subject-matter of *The Dawn in Britain* covers a vast field, both in time and space. The scene shifts between Britain, Italy, and Palestine, and the story extends from the first invasion of Britain by its primitive Celtic settlers to the destruction of Jerusalem by Titus. Yet, what appears, at first sight, no more than a long, legendary chronicle, has really an epic unity of its own, and in all this great mass of material, the leading themes are closely knit together. It is the struggle between Roman civilization and heroic barbarism, and the advent of Christianity, which really forms the subject of the poem. Thus, the first important episode is the sack of Rome by Brennus, who is represented as a British king; and later we are told of the descent of the Second Brennus upon the shrine of Apollo at Delphi. In these incidents we see barbarism triumphant over the nascent civilization of the south, which is later to subdue it. Much of the central part of the epic is occupied with the story of Caradoc (Caractacus) and his heroic but hopeless stand against the invading Romans. For the purposes of the poem Caradoc is made the ally and brother-in-arms of the Germanic chief, Thorolf, who is to be the ancestor of the Anglo-Saxons. Thus, both Celtic and Teutonic worlds are brought into relation as the common enemies and victims of Rome, and a connection with the future history of Britain is suggested.

Perhaps the most powerful single passage in the poem is that which deals with the agony of Caradoc in the hour of his despair, after he has received the news of Thorolf's death. He leaves his banqueting hall, and goes forth alone to muse on death and human fate, in the burying-place of his ancestors:

> Can muse
> The warlord's heavy heart; where have their being,
> Beneath, or in what circuit of yond stars,
> Disbodied souls! and what is that which saith
> An antique funeral chant of Verulam druids?
> Spent spirits, rekindled, at the Light, above,
> Revert, from stars, to be new bodies' guests:
> And other hymn, Are men the living dead!
> But who lie, gaping upright, in the grave,
> Whose rottenness we rue; ben not their deaths,
> (Night-sleep, this iron griesly grip, which hath
> None wakening, clod laid under clodded earth,)
> Surcease of burdens, and of every pain,
> Less grievous than our life, which yet, the sun
> See'th; that, like shaft's flight, tossed in every blast,
> Whereon, again, the woundless air doth close:
> Or like as tainted footstep, in this snow,
> Soon fading; which, therewith, doth utterly perish!
> But, and when cometh aught thing, of good, to us,
> Is that a seldom grace! King Caradoc felt
> His heart, like burning coal, in his cold breast,
> For Thorolf's death, his brother, in Mainland.

This passage works up to a terrifying climax, in which a powerful picture of a pagan universe, where the soul

13

of man is hemmed in by hostile or indifferent powers, is realized:

> Him-seemeth now left, alone, in a dead world,
> Mongst these unbound. Such, on his weary spirit,
> Then darkness falls, him-thought, ceased heavenly stars,
> To shine above: and sighed Caractacus:
> We perish, praying to insenate gods!
> Are men ungodly? ben not ye, O proud gods,
> Inhuman! or have ye no power to save?
> (When gods, their faces, turn away from us;
> Must not mishappen thing we undertake;
> That, groping, few life-days, still wrestling pass!)
> Ye careless stars, which shine, in chambered night,
> Shield-hall of heaven, like cierges clear; whereon
> Hang fates of men; and ye indeed be gods,
> Rid us of Roman strange invading enemies!
> Him-seemed, then his own soul, in waking vision,
> In likeness see of caged small writhing vivern,
> (The cognisance of great Cunobelin's house,)
> And peeping gods, gigantic visages,
> Which balefires, mocking, kindle him around.

Finally madness falls upon Caradoc. He hears the cry of wolves echoing through the frozen woods. Imagining them to be Romans, were-wolves, and their wolf-suckled kings —he rushes upon these fancied enemies. He hacks frenziedly with his sword at the forest trees, and falls at last exhausted and unconscious.

It is at this point that Doughty, by way of dramatic relief, shows his astonishing power of creating a mythology of his own, which seems entirely convincing and appropriate to his material.

> Like to some swart vast fowl, how silent Night,
> (As Day she covered, with her dusky wings,)
> Broods o'er dim sullen round, of earth and woods!
> It night of the moon-measurer of the year,
> Is, wherein, Belisama, eyebright goddess,

Girded in kirtle blue, with woodwives sheen,
Wont to fare forth; and her shield-maidens' train,
And loud hounds, in the forest-skies above.
She, Caradoc seeing, stays her aery wain:
And, marvelling! in cloud-cliff, her divine team
She bound: so lights this faery queen, benign,
(Like her sire Belin,) to the kin of men.
She goddess, leaning on her spear-staff, wakes
In this his loneness, in cold midnight grove,
Over the hero's sleep: and, in herself,
Quoth; what is blind, brief, discourse of man's life,
But as a spark, out of eternal Night;
Then shines as gladeworm, in the world, a moment:
Or glairy path of snail, which in the sun,
Glisters an hour; the next, of dew or rain,
Is molten. Like to hart, of a great horn,
Fallen in some hunter's pit lies here King Caradoc,
Man best beloved, mongst Britons, of all gods!
Yet is, of mortal wights, an old said saw;
Is worth no weal, who may no woe endure.
Sith, with her shield-brim, she traced round him, sleeping,
A circuit: wherein enter, him to hurt,
Might sprite, nor wight, nor beast, nor element!

Belisama is a perfectly living and genuine creation of the poetic imagination. Doughty had only her name, on some Romano-British inscription, as a hint upon which to build. She combines the characteristics of the classical Artemis with those of the fairy-queen of Northern folk-lore, and is perfectly appropriate to the setting. She is the symbol of the tenderness and beauty which seemed to be in Nature, and which served to alleviate man's sufferings, even though he may be unconscious of their operation. She brings to Caradoc's pagan universe a promise of Grace.

But concurrently with this picture of the gradual conquest by Rome of the barbarian world, Doughty treats of the coming of Christianity. This subject is treated with great simplicity, and when the scene is laid in Palestine, Doughty is able to draw upon his own direct knowledge of the civilization of the Near East. The central figure in these parts of the poem is Joseph of Arimathea. Doughty follows the mediæval tradition of Joseph's voyage from Palestine to Gaul and thence to Britain, where he planted the beginnings of a Christian Church. He omits, however, any reference to the Holy Grail legend, which is associated with these traditions —partly, doubtless, because he shrank from employing a symbol too closely linked in the minds of his readers with the half-comprehending romanticism of Tennyson, partly because the sacramental implications of that symbol lay outside his range of sensibility.

The climax of the poem is reached in the twenty-third book with the marriage of the Roman knight Pudens with his British bride Rosmerta, who is a convert to Christianity, and who takes the Roman name of Claudia. (This is the Claudia mentioned in St. Paul's Second Epistle to Timothy, who is believed by commentators to have been a British lady.) With this marriage Rome, Britain, and Christianity are reconciled, and the seeds of the new civilization of Britain, which is to spring from these three roots, are planted. The poem concludes with various episodes which, apparently unconnected, symbolize in different ways the death of the old world. Boadicea's rebellion, the last rally of the Britons, is crushed. Mona, the sacred island of the pagan druids, is laid waste by Agricola. Caradoc dies in exile in Rome, after having witnessed the burning of the city under Nero. Jerusalem is destroyed by Titus; and, finally, Joseph, his mission accomplished, is shown a vision of the future Christian Britain, and returns to die in Canaan. The poet concludes:

> Dear foster Muse, fails now my breath.

—a line moving in its simplicity; though the reader, remembering it is the last line of one of the longest poems in the English language, may afford a smile.

It is important to emphasize that *The Dawn in Britain* is

not to be dismissed as a mere curiosity, or an excursion into an
archaic dream-world like that of Morris. In depicting ancient
Britain, Doughty has penetrated so deeply into the sensibility of the most ancient poets that he gives us what is
eternal. Nor does he sentimentalize; his precision and realism
in describing slaughter and sacrifice, funeral pyre or Roman
triumph, is altogether admirable. His pictures of landscapes
and sea voyages are typical of his method. He gives us what
are recognizable as the unchanging features of Britain, but
with a freshness and clearness as though they were seen for
the first time, under the light of primitive suns, before the
hand of man could much alter or defile them. Thus the poem,
though apparently remote from ordinary experience, really
conveys an image of our own country, seen *sub specie aeterni-
tatis*, and of that slow and gradual progress from lower to
higher modes of existence which, for Doughty at least, is
History.

Doughty's attitude was fundamentally religious, but it is
not Christian. For him, all mythologies and religious systems
were true—attempts on the part of the human imagination
to give form to the eternal. Christianity represented the
latest and most nearly perfect of these attempts. Hence, the
anthropomorphic Celtic and other gods who play their part
in *The Dawn in Britain* have a divine reality of their own and
are not mere abstractions or decorative figures. But they
have a sort of impassivity, and are aloof from the sufferings of
mortal men. Doughty invents myths for himself, or imitates
from the Roman and Greek poets, with perfect freedom; and
no sense of incongruity is felt in his doing so. Yet when the
Christian myth is introduced and the story of the first
missionaries' triumph in Britain is related, the pagan gods
begin to take on a sinister aspect. Spenser alone, with the half-
Christian, half-pagan Platonism of the Renaissance, could in
like manner combine Christian and pagan mythology in the
same poem without giving the impression of inconsistency.

In his treatment of Christianity, we note that it is the

humanizing side of that religion which he emphasizes. He was, indeed, a liberal humanist holding to the broad Victorian belief in the gradual progress of Man, and the ultimate unity of all religions in a universal faith. This idea is developed more fully in his later allegory, *Mansoul*. The subject of *Mansoul*, which must be pronounced very much less successful than *The Dawn in Britain*, is a descent into the Underworld to search for the spirits of the great teachers of mankind. It concludes with a vision of the ideal city of humanity. Two other later poems, which are in the form of dramas—*The Cliffs* and *The Clouds*, both written before the Great War of 1914–1918—have a contemporary setting and are remarkable as envisaging the invasion of Britain from the air by the "Eastlanders". In *The Titans* the problem of the relation of Man to the machines he has created is made the subject of an allegorical myth.

In his use of language Doughty is more of a "modern" poet than any of his contemporaries, except Hopkins (though the latter, who had read *Arabia Deserta*, seems to have fallen into the error of dismissing it as no more than a piece of pseudo-Elizabethan archaism). Read slowly and carefully Doughty is never obscure, but in reaction against the verbose and rhetorical tradition which had overspread English poetry, he creates for himself a new syntax which is nevertheless a logical development of the native genius of the spoken language. In this revolutionary reaction of his thought upon his form he may be compared with Hopkins and also with Rimbaud. Like them, he presents words in such a way that their effect upon the sensuous imagination is greatly enhanced, and his visual images especially are of an astonishing clearness. In comparing him with Hopkins, however, it must always be borne in mind that Doughty is aiming at a balanced, objective, epic style, whose chief virtue must be narrative clarity, and in which archaisms are consciously employed to enhance the ritual effect. His poetry conveys itself, like that of his master Spenser, or a mediæval narrative poet, not by intensity of conceit or metaphor, but by the slow building-up, through the precise use of pictorial words, of the scene which he is describing. Such a poetry cannot be sampled in snatches or adequately represented by extracts. It must be read at leisure in order that its full power may be felt.

Doughty and Bridges are two rather isolated figures standing apart from the main stream of the Aesthetic Movement. Nevertheless they employed elements inherent in it—in the one case its Primitivism, and in the other its implied Idealism —and combined them with features of the Spenserian tradition of English poetry to construct, towards the close of their long lives, poems conveying a larger and reasoned view of the universe, such as their pre-Raphaelite forerunners lacked. Both were successful, though I believe Bridges's achievement to be on a much smaller scale than Doughty's. The central tradition of the Aesthetic Movement, however, developed into that poetry which is essentially characteristic of the 'nineties—the work of Ernest Dowson, Lionel Johnson, and others, among whom was the young W. B. Yeats.

Of this group I have already had occasion to say something, and it need not detain us long. Their work represents a low ebb in the tide of English verse. Fundamentally, the style of these poets is Swinburnian, though they derive their melody rather from some of the slighter verses among the later *Poems and Ballads* than from Swinburne's better-known, more noisy and flamboyant manner. In *A Ballad of Dreamland*, for example, we find Swinburne already approximating closely to the muted manner of Dowson:

> I hid my heart in a nest of roses,
>   Out of the sun's way, hidden apart;
> In a softer bed than the soft white snow's is,
>   Under the roses I hid my heart.
>   Why should it sleep not? why should it start,
> When never a leaf of the rose-tree stirred?
>   What made sleep flutter his wings and part?
> Only the song of a secret bird.

The 'nineties poets retain much of the pre-Raphaelites's affected archaism of diction, with its accompanying vagueness and loss of vitality. They have learned nothing of the lucidity of French poetry, though they have studied Baudelaire and Verlaine. Although they aim at a compressed and polished style, the proportions of words to thought in their work is very high. They are too much isolated from life for a real conception of the meaning of style to be possible for them.

It would not be unfair to say, I think, that they merely played at being poets. They sought to bring realities into their verse which the official Victorian tradition had excluded—the Music Hall, the Harlot's House—but they do this with a self-conscious air of naughtiness only; there is no attempt to assess the imaginative significance of these things. Some of them pursued paths of experience which society condemned as immoral or perverse, in life as well as in art—but here also, it was with a curious emotional immaturity. Though the fates of some of them were miserable, it is hard to-day to discern real tragedy in their story; and there is a like quality of unreality in the expression which others give to a religious conversion—though we need not, on that account, necessarily doubt their personal sincerity.

We must not, however, be too hasty in condemning the poets of the 'nineties because they separated art from morality and, therefore, from life. The picture of the universe offered by nineteenth-century materialism, and morality interpreted by industrial capitalism, could provide no imaginative framework upon which great poetry might be erected. The scepticism which was thus induced had led Walter Pater to formulate his "epicurean" doctrines. For him, the moment of aesthetic experience remained the only incontestable evidence of a reality beyond the material. His theories, vulgarized by Wilde and others, formed the basis of the *fin de siècle* artists' attitude. But these men did nothing to develop these theories, or to convert that mere attitude

into anything more. They were not prepared to be revolu-
tionaries, or to reassess the "reality" of the society in which
they found themselves, in terms of the aesthetic discoveries.
By implication, by their personal confessions, their cultivation of the sweets of sin, they accepted the morality which
they defied. There is a sneer in one of Wilde's books at the
respectability of some aristocratic spinister who "is always
making ugly things for the poor". Wilde's aesthetic sense
prompted him to detest the morality which involved the
making of ugly things for the poor, but he was unable to see
that this kind of "charity" was not really moral at all, and
that this apparent discrepancy between aesthetic and ethical
values implied a defect in the whole constitution of the
society in which he lived.

One among the poets of this group attempted a revolt.
Had John Davidson possessed a more congenial background,
and had circumstances permitted the fuller development of
his talent, he might have been more than an oddly frustrated
and unequal minor poet. As it was, internal conflict and
poverty drove him to suicide. The other members of the
Rhymers' Club were, for the most part, either dead or silent
by the turn of the century. The literary atmosphere of
England was becoming too close for the poet of individual
imagination to survive, and the advent of Kipling, "The
Singer of Empire", might seem a sinister portent.

The two women who wrote under the name of "Michael
Field" hold a somewhat anomalous position in the history of
the Aesthetic Movement. They have a good deal in common
with the poets of the 'nineties, but the influence of Browning
is also discernible, and gives to their work rather more
strength and depth. In their treatment of Greek subjects,
they succeed in capturing more of the genuine feeling
of the ancient world than do most of their contemporaries. They were markedly natural pagans; but after
their conversion to Roman Catholicism, a curious synthesis
of pagan and Christian images seems to be hinted at in their

verse—Christ and the Virgin move through the poems with
the grace of Aphrodite and Dionysus. If it were not for the
misdirected energy which led them to put most of their best
work into dramas laboriously carved out of Gibbon's
Decline and Fall, and their failure (too common among
women poets) completely to subdue their form to their
emotions, we might cite them as furnishing a pointer from
Aestheticism to a wider poetic vision.

An interesting phenomenon of the latter part of the century is that neglected poet, Wilfrid Scawen Blunt, whose
first poems appeared in the 'eighties, but who lived on till
1922. This champion of Egyptian Nationalism, in active and
practical rebellion against British Imperialism, is almost the
only legitimate heir of Byron among English poets. The
Byronic, individualistic, aristocratic rebel, actively concerned
in public affairs and in revolt against authority, had been
almost the normal type of romantic poet in Continental
countries—especially in Russia and Spain, where authority
had been most repressive. In England, where Byron himself
has been generally underrated, this type found little scope.
Authority, after the accession of Queen Victoria, was liberal
and enlightened; the prosperity brought to the country, first
by the Industrial Revolution, later by Imperialist expansion,
prevented social unrest from reaching its crisis in revolution,
above whose tide the militant individualist might for a
moment show his head.

Blunt's poetry has not the same improvisatory quality as
Byron's, but at its best it has something of his masculine,
athletic movement, and the same engaging frankness. Like
Byron, Blunt is possessed by a passionate, unreasoned feeling
of revolt, not only against human tyranny, but against the
whole constitution of the universe. He cries:

> I never yet could see the sun go down
> But I was angry in my heart. . . .
> What have we done to thee, thou monstrous Time?
> What have we done to Death, that we must die?

It is easy to dismiss this attitude as immature; but it expresses something which ultimately troubles all of us. Without this spirit of discontent, mankind could achieve nothing.

The same qualities are seen in Blunt's best poem, *Esther*. It is a short novel in verse, constructed as a series of sonnets. It tells how a very young, very proud, very bitter but strangely innocent young man falls in, quite by chance, with Esther, a strolling actress, whom he meets at a fair in Lyons. They live together for a time, perfectly happy, and then she leaves him:

> He who has once been happy is for aye
>   Out of destruction's reach. His fortune then
> Holds nothing secret, and Eternity,
>   Which is a mystery to other men,
> Has like a woman given him its joy.
>   Time is his conquest. Life, if it should fret,
> Has paid him tribute. He can bear to die.

That is all. Yet, somehow, it is extraordinarily moving. The frankness with which passion is treated contrasts strongly with the usual Victorian sentimentality, and with the self-conscious naughtiness of the 'nineties.

The muscular vigour of Blunt's style has some affinity with that developed by Yeats in his middle years. The poetic genealogy of Yeats was very different, though he, likewise, became an active rebel and was of aristocratic temperament. In his poetic development Yeats illustrates the ultimate end of one line of poetic evolution, and carries the Symbolist and Aesthetic traditions, and the greater Romantic tradition from which they sprang, down to our own times.

There is no question that the earlier work of Yeats is a direct and typical product of the Aesthetic Movement of the 'nineties. He was a member of the Rhymers' Club, and he had been introduced to Wilde. Through his friend Arthur Symons he became acquainted with the poetry of the French Symbolists, and he was brought by him to some of Mallarmé's little gatherings of poets in his Paris apartment. Villiers de L'Isle Adam's drama *Axel* made a profound impression on him. The pre-Raphaelites—Morris and Rossetti—both in poetry and painting, had seemed to him figures of first-rate importance, standing for the beginning of a new kind of art in England—an art in reaction against the bourgeois utilitarianism which he hated. His childhood had been nourished on Shelley and Spenser—Spenser, that fountain-head of the central Romantic tradition in England, and a Shelley appreciated not as the singer of Godwinian political justice, but as one who dealt in dream symbols and a quasi-Platonic mysticism.

Now it is often claimed in our days that the great qualities of Yeats's later verse were due to his repudiation of Aestheticism, and his turning, under stress of political preoccupations, to a new "realist" conception of poetry. This, I believe, is untrue. The aesthetic attitude remained to the last dominant with Yeats, and conditioned his political approach. But his Irish Protestant background, as well as his individual genius, prompted him to carry Aestheticism further than any of his English contemporaries, until it became modified into something apparently different.

It was this Anglo-Irish background which from the first differentiated Yeats from his fellow members of the Rhymers' Club. The Symbolists, from Poe and Baudelaire onwards, had been in revolt against the democratic ideals of the nineteenth century. Like Villiers de L'Isle Adam, they glorified the past and an aristocratic form of society. Among the pre-Raphaelites, Morris was an active Socialist, but he, too, looked to the past, and sought to revive ancient heroic legend, and the traditional culture of the folk. In his own Ireland, with its "hard-riding country gentlemen", and its peasantry, with their still living traditions of pre-Christian origin and of the ancient heroes, Yeats thought he could discern a living image, though perhaps a faded one, of the ideal world of the Aesthetic poets. When he allied himself with the Irish

Nationalist Movement—to which he was also drawn by his love for Maud Gonne—he hoped to see his aesthetic conception imposed upon the real political situation. Such a hope was, in the nature of things, doomed to frustration—and his last work, notably the play *Purgatory*, written not long before his death, shows how embittered he had become, and how disappointed with the new Ireland which had actually superseded the old; but he never abandoned his original ideas.

In *Purgatory*, two vagabonds, an old man and a young man, his son, stand before a ruined house which is haunted by the spirits of the dead, who there expiate their guilty lives. The last owner of the house, the heiress of an aristocratic family, had debased herself by marrying a drunken groom. This symbolizes the corruption of the old Anglo-Irish aristocracy which allowed itself to become contaminated by contact with the rising bourgeoisie. The old man, who represents the revolutionary generation, or Yeats himself, is the child of this union, now dispossessed of his heritage. His own son, who typifies the younger generation of the new Ireland, has his father's violence, but knows nothing of the traditions of the past for which Yeats himself cared so much. The play concludes with the killing of the younger man by his father.

Yeats declared himself a man of essentially religious nature who had been deprived of the use of the traditional symbols of belief by Huxley and the other scientific materialists of the nineteenth century. He sought to build for himself a new faith and a new system of symbols from his aesthetic experience—from the poetry of Shelley and Blake, Rossetti, Morris, and the Symbolists themselves. Later in the same way he drew upon what he could discover of the ancient mythology of the Celt. The setting forth on such a quest was typical of all those affected by the Aesthetic Movement, but Yeats carried it further than his contemporaries and predecessors. He sought also to discover the truth in theosophical occultism, adopted a belief in magic and paid great attention to dreams and the like. It seems to me that what he derived from theosophy, and indirectly from Indian religion, forms an intrusive element, and a somewhat tiresome one, in his poetry. Yeats would like to have believed himself a genuine mystic, as his friend "A. E." may have been. It seems probable that he falsely claimed for himself visions and supernatural experiences which had not really occurred to him. He finally produced in *A Vision*, which he stated had been dictated by spirits, his wife acting as the "medium", something like a complete philosophy of history and human psychology, based primarily on aesthetic conceptions and stated in abstract terms. This prose treatise, with its elaborate schematization, is a strange and in many ways a sterile work, though illuminated by flashes of profound insight. It is of great value for the light it throws on Yeats's mature position, but it has, in fact, little to do with poetry—which is a very different thing from magic and from mysticism as Yeats understood them.

The greatness of Yeats as a poet lay in his reassertion and rediscovery of the concrete; and this arose mainly from his enlarging his aesthetic scheme of the universe to bring the Irish political crisis within its scope. It was his love for Maude Gonne which drew him into this struggle. This love was, doubtless, the most powerful emotion of his life, and presented him with a paradox which much of his poetry is an attempt to solve. In his later poems he repeatedly compares her to Helen of Troy. Her beauty seemed to him to belong to a heroic past, and to have the proud, cold, and aloof quality which he most admired. Yet she herself was not thus impassive and aloof, but ready to throw herself whole-heartedly into the popular struggle, with what seemed to Yeats the sacrifice of individual integrity which that involved. She was not to become Yeats's wife, but she sought to induce him to use his poetic gifts in the interests of the cause with which she identified herself. Yeats's early work is a poetry of escape —escape as in *The Wanderings of Usheen*, into the other world of Celtic mythology. In the play, *The Shadowy Waters*, the hero Forgael and the queen Dectora, who becomes his lover, voyage unendingly over unknown seas, leaving humanity behind in search of this goal. But in *The Countess Cathleen* the heroine must sell her own soul to buy foods for her starving people. It is the image of Maude Gonne sacrificing herself for the Irish nation, and touches the heart of Yeats's personal problem as an Aesthetic poet. This play stands nearer to humanity, even to Christianity, than any of his other works; for in no other is the idea of self-sacrificing love involved.

But in his later years, Yeats's pursuit of aesthetic experience led him to further discoveries. He came to find once more the actual *beauty* of hard intellectual system, and of the commonplace—a knowledge the poets had steadily been losing sight of since the seventeenth century, and which the aesthetic poets had wholly set aside. In a late play, *The Words Upon the Window Pane*, in which the spirit of Swift manifests itself at a séance in modern Dublin, the eighteenth century is represented as the period when the human intellect reached its greatest heights. In many poems of his later years Yeats celebrates Swift, Berkeley, Goldsmith, and Burke as types of the great Protestant Irish tradition of which he himself was the last representative.

The Aesthetic philosophy which had taken the place of morals in art, Yeats began to apply to life. He became increasingly conscious of the sheer beauty of the life of the individual, untrammelled by social or ethical considerations. Men reached their highest stature in moments of proud defiance:

> A great man in his pride,
> Confronting murderous men.

Hence he found it necessary, in contradiction to Christian values, to exalt Pride above all other moral qualities, and in his latest poems—beginning with the "Crazy Jane" sequence—he exalted Lust in like manner. This was the logical conclusion of the neo-paganism which had entered English poetry with

Keats and Landor, but it must necessarily be shocking not only for Christians—but still more for those to whom it has never occurred to dispute the liberal humanitarian code (the legitimate child of Puritanism) of the nineteenth century.

Yeats confused aesthetics with morals, and magic with religion. The Symbolists had laid stress upon the incantatory power of words. The poem became a "charm", in the magical sense, and the poet a magician. The earlier Romantics had tended to see him as a prophet. Victor Hugo, whom Yeats admired, and who also dabbled, in his later years, in occult philosophy, is a prime example of this. Among the successors of the Symbolists the tendency was for the poet to become a mystagogue, the priest of a private religion. This role Yeats in Ireland, and, far more consistently and seriously, Stefan George in Germany, both adopted. Poetry became for them a means of self-exaltation, a method of obtaining spiritual power over others.

At the back of Yeats's poetry lies a philosophy of Power, not unakin to that of Nietzsche, who was also primarily an aesthetic thinker, and whom Yeats came greatly to admire. Such ideas were widespread in European culture at the time, and their connection with the genesis of Fascism—on however much of a lower level that political movement actually took shape—must not be glossed over.

That element is in Yeats's poetry, and it is more than skin deep. He had a romantic belief in aristocracy, and a contempt for "the butcher, the baker, the candlestick-maker"; he was embittered by his experience of the Irish revolution and its sequel. But, besides this, in his quest for an aesthetic synthesis, he came to exalt violence, and even cruelty, the instinctive and animal, over the human. When he envisaged the ideal state of the future he frankly enumerated the phenomenon of "great wealth in the hands of a few men" as among its characteristics. His poem *The Second Coming* has been interpreted as a prophecy of the advent of Fascism; but it is not clear that in this wonderful poem the "rough beast" which "slouches towards Bethlehem to be born" is regarded as an enemy—rather it is looked upon as a new Redeemer who comes to inaugurate an era of violence and inhumanity, which the poet himself accepts and even welcomes.

Left wing or Liberal critics have either shut their eyes to this element in Yeats's poetry, or have been rendered very uneasy by it. They would like to deny to Yeats, as a "reactionary", his just place as the greatest of modern poets in the English language. But this is impossible; no honest critic of any sensibility can fail to mark his superiority, not only in his own generation, but over any poet who has so far succeeded him.

In the two poems, *Byzantium* and *Sailing to Byzantium*, that imperial city becomes the symbol of Yeats's other world of aesthetic experience, to which, after death, his soul is to go, taking the form of a gold mechanical singing bird in the Emperor's garden—"a work of art producing works of art", as has been well remarked. The sensuous island paradise, derived from Celtic legend, which appears in the early poems—such as *The Happy Townland*—has given place to this great image. Everything in Byzantium suggests hardness or violence. The sages standing in the fire, in the gold mosaic of a wall, the blood-begotten spirits, the Emperor's drunken soldiery.

That dolphin-torn, that gong-tormented sea.

—all these, at the same time as they evoke the static beauty of a world of perfected art. This is the ideal existence to which Yeats is so strongly drawn, and in terms of life it implies a deliberate and heartless régime of oppression in the cause of beauty.

It is difficult for those who have inherited no tradition but that of nineteenth-century bourgeois Liberalism to understand the strength of the temptation which the vision of Byzantium represents. They cannot realize how often democratic ideals have blurred the vision of beauty which the artist apprehends, or sacrificed it to inadequate moral

14

considerations. They do not understand how much beauty there is, even in human violence and cruelty.

Instead of treating Yeats's poetry with reserve or hostility, these critics should submit themselves in spirit to his vision. They should be grateful to the poet who can show them the terrible image of Byzantium, and the power of its attraction. It was because the intellectual and emotional scope of their own philosophy was not wide enough, that so many were unexpectedly stampeded into the unreasoning reaction of Fascism. The progressive must realize the power and extent of the pure aesthetic hunger in the soul of man. Unless, in the world they are striving for, that hunger can also have satisfaction, Byzantium will persist as a potential enemy of the Just City.

But Yeats, as I have said, modified his aesthetic approach in so far as he tended more and more to exalt those beauties which he discovered in life, above those he had experienced in art. The *Dialogue of Self and Soul* takes us a stage further than the Byzantium poems. The Soul calls the poet away from life, by way of the winding stair of thought in the symbolic tower—not now to Byzantium or any paradise of the senses, but into the outer darkness of death, the unknown absolute. But the Self, seated with the ancestral sword, symbol of war and conflict, upon his knees, and the embroidery which wraps it, symbol of love and beauty, finally rejects that temptation. The old man thinks of his past life, where he has found that completest satisfaction of the senses which the aesthetic attitude calls for, and he cries:

> I am content to live it all again
> And yet again, if it be life to pitch
> Into the frog-spawn of a blind man's ditch,
> A blind man battering blind men;
> Or into that most fecund ditch of all—
> The folly that man does
> Or must suffer, if he woos
> A proud woman not kindred to his soul.

I am content to follow to its source
Every event in action or in thought;
Measure the lot; forgive myself the lot!
When such as I cast out remorse
So great a sweetness flows into the breast
We must laugh and we must sing,
We are blessed by everything,
Everything we look upon is blessed.

It is to this final faith in the blessedness of life and of matter that the following of the guidance provided by his aesthetic intuition, uninhibited by moral considerations, has brought Yeats. It may be that his passionate love of beauty rendered him in his generation an embittered old man and a reactionary, but perhaps we can accept his faith in life without travelling the dangerous road that brought him to it. For, if we believe in the capacity of humanity to be redeemed, and that it is in this material existence that the work of redemption takes place, we need not shrink from any experience which the senses and the imagination may offer us. No poetry which satisfies our intellect and our senses together will, on ultimate examination, prove false.

At any rate, that is the faith in which this book has been written.

INDEX

INDEX